THE
POSSIBLE
IMPOSSIBILITIES

JOYCE SMITH-MOORE, N.D.

First Edition: May 2017

Library of Congress
Joyce Smith-Moore, N.D.
The Possible Impossibilities - 1st ed.

**Library of Congress
ISBN – 13: 9781548163075**

Comments about *The Possible Impossibilities* and requests for additional copies are available on amazon.com. Speaking appearances may be addressed to Joyce Smith-Moore, N.D. at 2 Loop Rd., Suite 702, Auburn, NY 13021. E-mail address is: drjasmith@zoho.com

Printed in the United States of America.

DEDICATED TO:

MY SON, ASHLEY AND GRANDSON, STEPHEN BOTH DIED TRAGICALLY AT THE AGE OF 17.

&

*dedicated also to those who are the 'rare gems' in my life
... family & friends who made a big difference
and who truly are "exceptions to the rule"...*

FAMILY

IRENE "NAY NAY" BERNHEISEL
JONATHAN HACKETT
JAMES R. MOORE
JENNIE LIND DOWNEY
ALDEN D. WARD

FRIENDS

JOAN & LOREN BLACKBURN
DENNIS "CHUCK" COLE
VICTORIA FALLET
BARRIE GEWANTER
BOURKE KENNEDY
FLORENCE LANSDOWNE
NANCY CHENEY-NETTI
RON VAN NOSTRAND
MARY OSGOOD
RICHARD RYMPH
EMERALD "EMMA" SMITH
DR. LAVONA STILLMAN
FLORENCE WALKER
"JACKIE" WENTWORTH
DONNA WURTZ
REV. MAE MERRIT YORK

BASIC PRINCIPLES OF SPIRITUALISM

1. We believe in the Fatherhood of God and the Brotherhood of man.
2. All Phenomena that occur within the realms of nature, both physical and spiritual, are manifestations of Infinite Intelligence.
3. True religion is discovered by understanding correctly the Laws of Nature and of God, and by living in harmony therewith.
4. Individual existence, personal identity and memory continue after the transitional experience called death.
5. Communication with the "Living Dead" is a scientific fact, fully proven under test conditions by the phenomena of psychical research. (IONS)
6. The Golden Rule, "Whatsoever ye would that others should do unto you, do ye also unto them," is the essence of morality.
7. Every individual is morally self-responsible. Happiness flows from consonance with the Laws of Nature and God.
8. The genuine improvement and reformation of the human soul are always possible in this world and the next.
9. Prophecy exists in our times as in Biblical Days and is proven scienficially through mediumistic powers of divination ... *now called: "channeling"*
10. The Universe, as a spiritual system expressing Divine Wisdom, makes possible the external progress of the aspiring soul who loves truth and goodness.

+ + + + + + + + + + + + + + + + +

"THE POSSIBLE IMPOSSIBILITIES"

TABLE OF CONTENTS

page no.

(*) The term 'Noetic' derives from the Greek word for 'mind'. Noetic scientists study whether age old ideas like – *faith healing, ESP, mind over matter* – actually have a scientific basis.

The play "Circles" written by the author of this book and performed by the Auburn Community Players in 2008 was taken from the 1894 article: "Voices From The Grave" and 'excerpts' of said news article appear in the last chapter of this book. The article provides an accounting of what was actually witnessed by that writer ... proof of what 'spirits' are capable of doing ... that was also witnessed by credible individuals who sat in those 'circles'.

FOREWORD

Einstein said, "The most beautiful and most profound emotion we can experience is the sensation of the mystical. It is the sower of all true science. He to whom this emotion is a stranger, who can no longer wonder and stand rapt in awe, is as good as dead." (Quote taken from Lincoln Barnett's book: "The Universe and Dr. Einstein." New York: Bantam Books, 1957, pg. 108.)

+ + + + + + + + + + + + + +

Not since internationally renowned thanatologist Dr. Elizabeth Kubler-Ross's *(1969)* book "Death and Dying" has another been written that connects to what began a century ago as *Spiritualism.* And … if I don't write how they now connect, then I don't know who will!

And, despite most believing it has minimal historical importance, it is nevertheless necessary to enlighten those interested readers to what is the truth about what really happened in Auburn, New York where it really began … and so, what follows is what supports its beginnings.

I am also certain that my early childhood experiences of seeing ghosts *(aka: 'spirits' or 'lost souls')* had a lot to do with my later investigation and pursuit of finding proof of it.

GHOSTS: *Most call them "ghosts" but they should, instead, be referred to as either "earth-bound spirits" or "lost souls". The reasons many do not progress ..."go to the light" ... are numerous. Many are stuck because they are unprepared to die. There are also those who stay "earth bound" because of their while-on-earth addictions. And, for those who were electrocuted, they usually remain as "earth-bound spirits".*

In the 1970s, I had the rare opportunity to train with a well-known and also, one of the oldest living *"mediums"* at that time - the Rev. Mae Merritt York. *(She and Arthur Ford worked the circuit in the 1930s, drawing huge crowds at the Spiritualist Campgrounds in Freeville, New York, similar to the way television medium Jonathan Edwards does today.)*

In the process of beginning my research into *Spiritualism* in the 1970s, I was surprised to discover that the first gathering of people interested in this phenomenon occurred in 1849, in my hometown of Auburn, New York. They met regularly in the homes of some of Auburn's most prominent citizens. They called themselves *"The Auburn Circle."* They included: Henry D. Barron, Mary and Charles W. Bennet, James H. and Sarah Bostwick *(J. H. Bostwick was a surveyor and, for a time, Auburn's police chief)*, Lucio Gardner, Martha A. Hilman, Miss Amanda Hoskins, Dewitt C. and Mary Miller, Dr. Haratio Robinson, Sr. *(a physician)*, Dr. Sullivan N. Smith *(a dentist)*, Henry Sheffield, Mr. and Mrs. Justin Sturtevant, S.A. Tamlin, Haratio N. Thompson, Ethan A. Warden, George S. Wilson and C.V. Woodward.

Always in attendance was ten-year-old Catherine Fox. (She and her younger sister, Maggie, were already beginning to get national and world-wide attention with the "rappings" that occurred during their public "seances." More about the girls is included in a subsequent chapter.)

Documented as the homes where *'circles'* were held in Auburn included: Dr. and Mrs. Robinson – 6 William Street; Mr. And Mrs. James Boswick – 172 W. Genesee Street; Dr. and Mrs. Sullivan Nortan Smith – 148 W. Genesee Street; Mr. And Mrs. Dewitt Miller – 25 South Street; and C.V. Woodward – 120 North Street.

(The Cayuga County Office Building occupies where the Boswick home once stood and the Veterans' Park is on the site where the Smith home stood. The only home still standing today is the white columned home on North Street.)

By 1870, the Auburn area was home to more than 100 *mediums*. It was only after Mary Todd Lincoln's trip to Auburn in February 1872, to see the *medium* Mary Andrews in nearby Moravia, that the town became known as *The Mecca of Spiritualism*. Her trip increased the popularity of *mediums*, as evidenced by the eight trains that made the 17-mile trip from Auburn daily to Moravia.

MY OWN EXPERIENCE(S) AS A 'MEDIUM'

Although I've witnessed hundreds of *mediums"* doing *readings* over several decades, I am aware that the help I've been given by *'the other side'* has been much greater than given to those others. I am also aware of the fact that I am truly not the best. There's Blavatsky and Nostradamus … and so many others who've proved themselves!

MEETING STEPFANY ANNE GOLBERG

Stepfany Anne Golberg is a well-known writer on the topic. I met her during the Summer of 2013. This is what she included in her article *"Give Up The Ghost":*

"In the Cayuga-Owasco Lakes Historical Society, Moravia's resident historian and one of its last remaining Spiritualists, sits in her office cheerfully drawing pies on the backs of fundraiser mailings. Her museum is a single darkish room dedicated to Moravia's most prominent citizen, Millard Fillmore, whose life is showcased with dusty family memorabilia and miscellaneous local items thrown in for

filler. In a corner of the room, blocked off by dividers next to the kitchen, is a little exhibit of Xeroxed pictures and newspaper articles providing a short history of <u>Spiritualism</u>. It is a presentation of a strange and forgotten movement, and of a country's existential crisis. The ghosts are sleeping now, the exhibit says, but they could stir at any moment."

Most of what Stepfany Anne Golberg wrote in her 2013 magazine article about *Spiritualism* is accurate.

Her reference to my being Moravia's *"resident historian"* is inaccurate. Yes, I am a *historian* but I am not the town's *"resident historian"*. The title belongs to another person. Her mentioning my "drawing pies on the backs of fundraiser mailings" should *(perhaps)* have been further explained since pies are often depicted for fund raising purposes and referred to as *"charts"*.

And, as it relates to the *"Millard Fillmore Exhibit"* ... her impression makes it sound like a ghastly one! My recommendation would be for the reader to go the Cayuga-Owasco Lakes Historical Society's website and judge it for oneself: <u>www.colhs.org/p/about-HTML</u>

(The COLHS organization houses the <u>only</u> exhibit of our 13th U.S. President's personal effects and memorabilia. A statue of him is in front of the University of Buffalo's administration building because he was their first chancellor.)

Had Stepfany taken a closer examination into the City of Auburn's history she would not have said *"it was a new city built on the wealth of the Erie Canal"* ... because history indicates otherwise. *(The fact that she didn't dig deeper into Auburn's history is why she missed what I discovered years previously about the first "circles" (aka: "seances") being conducted in the homes of Auburn's elite!)*

How fortunate for me because I'm also able to do them! *(I've conducted well over one hundred 'circles' ... usually for non-profit 'fund raising' purposes that I never received any payment for doing.)*

There has also always been an assumption that it was only women who were drawn into *Spiritualism.* In Stefany's research she indicates otherwise. She lists the category of believers of *Spiritualism "as men being the primary defenders: politicians, physicians, scientists, writers, politicians, industrialists — white, prominent, educated, wealthy, Protestant."* Goldberg's conclusion is that *"Spiritualists fit weirdly in the story of America."*

Certainly it was the Civil War Period that this *new belief system* opened the door – *ever so slightly* – to what might be possible!

But it wasn't till 1969 when the door to darkness was *finally* opened – *all the way* – because of what world renowned psychiatrist, Dr. Elizabeth Kubler-Ross said:

"At the moment of transition, you're never, ever alone. You're never alone now, but you don't know it. But at the time of transition, your guides, your guardian angels, people whom you have loved and who have passed on before you, will be there to help you in this transition. This has been verified beyond any shadow of a doubt, and I say this as a scientist."

(Anyone who was trained as a nurse in the United States since 1980 is well aware of

Kubler-Ross's work and therefore, most of them are believers in the existence of a 'spirit world'.)

THANK YOU DR. KUBLER-ROSS FOR CONFIRMING WHAT IS THE TRUTH! AND, AS A RESULT ... I'M BEING ACCUSED A LOT FEWER TIMES OF BEING "CRAZY"!

In 2003, thanks to the efforts of Eileen McHugh, Director of the Cayuga Museum of History and Art in Auburn, New York a public exhibit of my documentation that supported the fact that "Auburn was the first city in America to have had 'circles' (aka: seances) held in it!"

And, according to what we now know about the growth of *Spiritualism* in Cayuga County, by 1870 Cayuga County was home to more than 100 *mediums. (And, no doubt President Millard Fillmore was also aware of the movement since he was a native of nearby Moravia.)*

It was after Lincoln's assassination that Fillmore more than likely told Mary Todd Lincoln about Mary Andrews since the *medium* was also a resident of Moravia and considered "the most famous *medium* in the region."

Two close acquaintances of Fillmore were advocates of the *movement* and also known to have consulted the *medium.* They were Mr. William Smith and Judge John Worth Edmonds. *(Smith was the founder of William Smith College in Geneva, New York. Judge Edmonds was the President of the Senate and Judge of the Supreme Court of New York. The judge's two-volume set of books on* Spiritualism *are not only among the best written on the subject, they are also hard to find.)*

It was on February 22, 1872 that Mary Todd Lincoln made the trip to see the *medium* Mary Andrews in Moravia and even spent the night in the Andrews' home before returning to Auburn on the train. She stayed another night at the National Hotel where she also consulted the clairvoyant physician, Dr. Hotaling. *(Mrs. Lincoln gave the doctor "credit of giving the best diagnosis of her case ever before given" according to The Auburn Daily Bulletin – 2/27/1872).*

The same news article tells of her visit to Moravia. The visit no doubt was the also the cause of further *'fanning the flames'* of the *Spiritualist movement*!

Lester Luther writes in his book: <u>Moravia and Its Past</u> that "almost immediately after her visit the town became known as <u>*The Mecca of* Spiritualism</u>, causing the town to prosper, as evidenced by livery stables and hotels which were always full."

+ + + + + + + + + + + + +

MORAVIA – THE MECCA OF SPIRITUALISM

The brochure I wrote when I was President of the Cayuga-Owasco Lakes Historical Society in 1990, "Moravia – The Mecca of Spiritualism" was the first ever written, acknowledging why the town had been given that 'title' in the late 1800s. The Cayuga Owasco Lakes Historical Society has realized all proceeds from the sale of the brochure. It was the intent of this writer to not only trace the history of the movement in the area and elsewhere ... but to further unfold the mysteries of 'Spiritualism'. (Much of what follows in this chapter is contained in that brochure.)

* * * * * * * * * * * * * *

Webster's Dictionary defines *"Spiritualism"* as *"the belief that the dead survive as spirits which can communicate with the living, especially with the help of a third party, called a 'medium'."*

Both the Old and New Testaments of the **Bible** talk about spirit intervention and communication from approximately 1800 B.C. to around 200 A.D. Throughout their pages the reader is *"warned to discriminate carefully between true and false,"* and many admonished to *"test the spirits."*

Even Jesus appeared eleven times after his death death upon the cross and tells the disciples *"there is no death ... life is everlasting."*

Over the centuries, death has drawn great scrutiny and a distinct turning away. Most preferred to shut the darkness out by keeping the door slammed to death!

But, all that changed in 1969 when psychiatrist Elizabeth Kubler-Ross's landmark book, *On Death and Dying* marked the beginning of the end of denial about what happens to us as we die. The following passage is taken from her book:

> *"At the moment of transition, you're never, ever alone. You are not alone right now, but you don't know it. At the time of transition, your spirit guides, your guardian angels, people whom you have loved and who have passed on before you, will be there to help you in this transition. We have verified this beyond any shadow of a doubt, and I say this as a scientist. Most of the time it is a mother or father, a grandparent, or a child if you have lost a child. It is sometime people that you didn't even know were on the other side."*

When astronaut Edgar Mitchell founded the Institute of Noetic Sciences (IONS) in 1971, the investigation of *"mediumship"* became one of the areas of focus for the Institute. A core group of their scientists and researchers eventually published a book on the subject and a new name was given to it called: *"Channeling"* – which is also the name of their book. Thus the *"stamp of approval"* was given to it and *"communication with the other side"* was recognized as possible!

But … before we go any further, we need to go back to a date in time when *Spiritualism* got its start in the United States on March 31, 1848.

Events which occurred for the Fox family in Hydesville, New York on that fateful March 31st evening in 1848 initiated the Modern Spiritualist Movement.

(At that time, Hydesville was a small hamlet near Newark and about 20 miles southeast of Rochester.)

Just three months earlier, in December of 1847, John Fox, along with his wife Margaret and their two daughters, Catherine *(called "Cathie" as a child and later, "Kate")* and Margaretta *(called "Maggie")*, moved into their temporary quarters while their own home was being built nearby.

They'd heard that the house had a reputation of being 'haunted' … in fact, they were aware that the prior tenant, Michael Weakman, moved out of the house because of it! However, it wasn't until mid-March that the Fox family began to be disturbed by unexplained sounds and activities.

The following is an accounting given in a signed affidavit by Mrs. Fox on April 11, 1848 of what had been occurring since mid-March.

"On the night of the first disturbance we all got up, lighted a candle and searched the entire house, the noises continuing during the whole time, and being heard near the same place. Although not very loud, it produced a jar of the bedsteads and chairs that could be felt when we were in bed. It was a tremendous motion, more than a sudden jar. We could feel the jar when we were standing on the floor. It continued on this night until we slept. I did not sleep until about twelve o'clock.

"On March 30th we were disturbed all night. The noises were heard in all parts of the house. My husband stationed himself outside the door while I stood inside, and the knocks came on the door between us. We heard footsteps in the pantry, and walking sounds downstairs; we could not rest, and I then concluded the house must be haunted by some unhappy restless spirit. I had often heard of such things, but had never witnessed anything of the kind that I could not account for before.

"On Friday night, March 31ˢᵗ ... my youngest child, Cathie, said: "Mr. Splitfoot, do as I do, 'clapping her hands'. The sound instantly followed her with the same number of raps. When she stopped, the sound ceased for a short time. Then Margaretta said, in sport, "Now, do just as I do. Count one, two, three, four," striking one hand against the other at the same time, and the raps came as before. She was afraid to repeat them.

"Then Cathie said in her childish simplicity, 'Oh, mother, I know what it is. Tomorrow is April-Fools day, and it's somebody trying to fool us'.

"I then asked: 'Is this a human being that answers my questions so correctly?' There was no rap. I asked: 'Is it a spirit? If it is, make two raps.' Two sounds were given as soon as the request was made. I then said: 'If it was an injured spirit, make two raps,' which were instantly made, causing the house to tremble. I asked: Were you injured in this house?' The answer was given as before. 'Is the person living that injured you?' Answered by raps in the same manner. I ascertained by the same method that it was a man, aged thirty-one years, that had been murdered in this house, and his remains were buried in the cellar; that his family consisted of a wife and five children, two sons and three daughters, all living at the time of his death, but that his wife had since died. I asked: 'Will you continue to rap if I call my neighbors that they may hear it too?' The raps were loud in the affirmative.

"My husband went and called in Mrs. Redfield, our nearest neighbor ... she came immediately (this was about half-past seven) ... she was amazed ... she then got her husband, and the same questions were asked and answered."

It was also ascertained that the spirit's name was Charles B. Rosna and that he had been a peddler who had stayed at the house five years previously.

THE MOVEMENT GROWS

With a view to satisfy himself on the subject, author Eliah
A. Capron of Auburn induced the parents of Catherine
(Kate) – then about twelve years old – to come to Auburn
during the summer of 1849 and spend several weeks with his
family in the home of Captain G.V. Bennet.

Kate's oldest brother David Fox lived in nearby Aurora.
He and Kate were the frequent dinner guests at the homes of
some of Auburn's most prominent citizens.

> *(There exists an 1850 map of Auburn in the
> Cayuga County Historian's office that shows the
> location of the five residences where the group
> met ... on William Street, Genesee Street and
> North Street. On those streets is where the
> homes of Auburn's "elite" lived. They called
> themselves "The Auburn Circle." And later,
> they changed the name of their group to: "The
> Apostolic Movement.")*

Members of the group included: Henry D. Barron, Mary
and Charles W. Bennet, Sarah and James H. Bostwick
(surveyor and for a time, Auburn's police chief), Eliah A.
Capron *(journalist/author)*, Lucio Gardner, Martha A.
Hilman, Miss Amanda Hoskins, Dewitt C. and Mary Miller,
Dr. Haratio Robinson, Sr. *(physician)*, Mr. Henry Sheffield,
Dr. Sullivan Nortan Smith *(dentist)*, Mr. and Mrs. Justin
Sturtevant, S.A. Tamlin, Haratio N. Thomson, Ethan A.
Warden, George S. Wilson *(printer)*, and C.V. Woodward.
Several "circles" *(later called – seances")* were held that
year and the next.

*(Four of the five homes are now gone. The two
residences on Genesee Street were torn down to make room
for the Cayuga County Office Building and the Veterans'
Memorial Park. The residence shown on William Street is
the present location of the YMCA. The Genesee Mall
building is on the site of where the fourth residence is shown
on the map on South Street. The only house still standing
where 'circles' were held is Mrs. C.V. Woodward's residence
on North Street.)*

Although Auburn became the first city in the nation to
conduct "circles", the first public demonstration of a
"seance" was held at the Corinthian Hall in Rochester, New
York, on November 14, 1849. The demonstration was
arranged by Mr. Eliah A. Capron of Auburn. Both of the Fox
sisters were on stage and demonstrated their ability to
"communicate" with "the other side"! *(About four hundred
attended the event and were greatly impressed and a great
deal of national publicity resulted.)*

For several years the Fox sisters drew big crowds
wherever they performed. Unfortunately what happened
when the cellar was dug up to a depth of about five feet, the
summer of 1848 … nothing was found! The 'occurrence' put
an almost immediate end to the media blitz which had been
occurring since Margaret Fox's statement had been given to
the press six months earlier.

+ +

THE 'PROOF' WAS FINALLY DISCOVERED

BUT IT CAME TOO LATE !

*It was not until 56 years later that a further discovery was
made which proved beyond all doubt that someone had
actually been buried in the cellar of the Fox household …
but found instead … behind the cellar wall!*

The following statement appeared in the **_Boston Journal_** *(a non-Spiritualist newspaper)* on November 23, 1904:

> *"Rochester, N.Y., Nov. 22, 1904: The skeleton of the man supposed to have caused the 'rappings' first heard by the Fox sisters in 1848 has been found in the walls of the house occupied by the sisters, and clears them from the only shadow of doubt held concerning their sincerity in the discovery of spirit communication."*

"The discovery was made by William H. Hyde, a reputable citizen of Clyde who owns the house and made an investigation. He found an almost entire human skeleton between the earth and crumbling of the walls and corroborates the sworn statement made by Margaret Fox, April 11, 1848."

One has to wonder what the significant differences might have been if that discovery had been made back then!

ELIAH A. CAPRON

Capron wrote in Chapter IV of his book, <u>*Modern Spiritualism*</u> that *"the number of mediums in Auburn, during the summer of 1850, increased very rapidly, until there were from fifty to one hundred in different stages of development."*

Both local newspapers, the local *Northern Christian Advocate* and the *Auburn Daily Advertiser* repeatedly *"attacked all who had anything to do with investigating the subject of Spiritualism."*

One of the area's most prominent citizens and for 40 years an advocate of the phenomena was William Smith. He built the Smith Opera House in Geneva in 1894. He once planned to establish a *Spiritualist* institution but instead, founded William Smith College in 1908 – the first non-denominational college in the United States.

It may be of interest to the reader to know that the author of this book was instrumental in beginning the restoration of the Smith Opera House in 1979. What the reader will discover in a subsequent chapter of this book is how – by a strange occurrence/coincidence – I learned that William Smith was a 'Spiritualist'!

What is also of importance about Mr. Smith is that he visited the *medium* Mary Andrews in Moravia and no doubt learned about her from the relatives of the Fillmores who had also grown up in the village.

KEELER'S HOUSE
Morris Keeler was a native of Cortland and moved to Moravia at the age of nine with his father, John Keeler. In 1830, he married Mary Abbott of Danbury, Connecticut. He was both a farmer and a businessman. Keeler was also instrumental in promoting the building of the *Southern Central Railroad*. It was later called the *Lehigh Valley Railroad.*
In 1860, Keeler hired a young woman by the name of Sarah "Mary" Meehan to be his housekeeper. She was from Auburn. He soon discovered she was able to communicate with the *"spirit world"* and so encouraged her in her *"mediumship"* development.

Seances were held in the Morris Keeler house on Oak Hill Road as early as 1830. In 1868 he rebuilt the house, and included a dark room for the sittings. The windows were covered with blankets and the shutters were closed so that it was as dark as midnight when the oil lamp was extinguished A cupola was added to the house. *(Apparently 'spirit' instructed Keeler to do this!)* Some believed that it was necessary to have a cupola in order for the spirits to be able to enter and depart the building. *(This is no longer a belief held by those who do 'channeling'.)* The house still stands today on Oak Hill Road. *(The 'cupola' was removed when new owners remodeled the house in 2010.)*

Sarah "Mary" Meehan married John Andrews and they moved into a house at the corner of North Main Street and Keeler Avenue. John was born in Moravia. He was a local businessman and the village trustee, a position he continued to hold for several years thereafter. He was also a member of the Moravia Fire Department and later served for a time as "Chief".

In the book, *Historical Sketches of Moravia (p. 379)*, John is given credit for being *"the first to undertake concrete construction in Moravia ... the cement walks all about the village attest to his handiwork ... as well as other village improvements."* Also indicated on that page, *"John showed little or no interest in his wife's vocation as a 'medium'; however, other than its pecuniary benefits."*)

As already mentioned previously, there were as many as eight trains belonging to the Southern Central Railroad that rolled into Moravia daily and a great many came because of Moravia's reputation. It is said that "thousands visited the *séance room* in the '*Spiritual Temple'* where *'circles'* were held almost every day. The town prospered, as evidenced by livery stables and hotels which were always full."

THE EXPANSION OF 'SPIRIUALISM' IN THE REGION

During the decades which followed, Spiritualists' church groups established summer campgrounds across the nation. A short distance from Moravia – in Freeville – one was set up by the *Central New York Spiritualist Association* in 1894 and is still in existence today. *(From 1976 to 1982, this author served on the board of the CNYSA.)*

The Freeville Campground hosted many prominent *'clairvoyants'* of the day, including Arthur Ford who Catholic Bishop Pike consulted on a number of occasions. *(It is well known that Bishop Pike was a dedicated but troubled believer in the Catholic Church and often found himself at odds with its beliefs and teachings which he considered out-of-date in some ways. He was popular in the turbulent period of the 1960's. When his plane went down in 1969 – while on a trip to Europe – it was Arthur Ford who "provided the exact longitude and latitude of where the plane went down!" Proof of that was reported in several European newspapers.)*

Since the late 1960s, attendance at Freeville has continued to decline. However, the Lily Dale Assembly located in southwestern New York State *(one hour southwest of Buffalo)* is an active Spiritualist Campground and each year several thousand visitors still come for classes, workshops, public church services and *mediumship* demonstrations, lectures, and private appointments with *mediums* who live on the grounds. .

Prominent *"speakers"* that have lectured at Lily Dale include Dr. Wayne Dyer, Dr. Deepen Chopra and

James Van Praagh. *(The author of this book has both lectured and been a 'guest' medium at Lily Dale.)*

THE HISTORY OF THE CASCADE HOTEL

The Cascade Hotel outside of Moravia existed in 1853 and was operated by H.D. Smith. Originally it was on the Auburn and Moravia Plank Road.

Lyman Soule, a known Spiritualist, bought the Cascade Hotel in 1867 from Robert P. Davis for $4,000. The parcel also included 53 acres of land. The following year, Soule sold it to Thomas M. Howe, another Spiritualist, for $5,000.

However, it was because of the railroad in the early 1870s that Cascade became a frequent stop because it was on Owasco Lake and became for many, a 'summer retreat'.

Around midnight on March 23, 1871, a chimney fire broke out and the hotel was destroyed. *(Fortunately everyone got out in time!)* A new and much larger hotel was quickly built, and in April 1872 Howe leased it for one year to William Bluefield of Syracuse. However, on April 23, 1873, Howe sold the Cascade Hotel and the land around it to John and Mary Andrews for $11,000. *(She is said to have earned $1,000. a month during the time she operated her "mediumship business" at the hotel!)*

Cascade was established as a post office on June 19, 1874, with John Andrews as the first postmaster. It was discontinued on May 15, 1904. Andrews leased the Cascade Hotel to Dr. E.S. Cleveland, M.D. of Rochester in 1894.

Cleveland described it as *"a resort site for people of all classes ... where they can find pleasure, rest and retirement from the cares of business."* He called it: "The Glen at Cascade". Bath houses and a picnic grove were built and additional recreational facilities were added.

It was on May 28, 1879, the Andrews sold the place to another Spiritualist, R.E. Schermerhorn of Rochester, who carried on the same traditions for a few more years.

It may be of interest to the reader to know that John D. Rockefeller often dined at the Cascade Hotel on his summer pilgrimages to his boyhood home near Moravia.

Another famous person, the gangster "Legs" Diamond was also an occasional visitor.

A famous boat, "The Lady of The Lake" brought frequent "guests" from the foot of the lake and followed the shoreline to Cascade. *(Later the "Enna Jettick Park" was built at the foot of the lake and became a major summer attraction until the advent of WWII.)*

Even Auburn's "Ted" Case, famed for his invention of the motion picture sound track *("lip sync")* brought his celebrity guests in his boat from his spacious home at Casowasco for impromptu parties at the Cascade Hotel because of its dance pavilion. *(How the author met Mr. Case – in the most unusual of circumstances – will be told about in a later chapter of this book.)*

Torn down in the 1950s, the wood salvaged from the Cascade Hotel was used to build the three camps that are presently on the site where the hotel once stood.

MRS. LINCOLN'S VISIT TO MORAVIA

It was Mary Todd Lincoln's trip to Moravia on February 22, 1872 which helped the town's reputation as *"The Mecca of Spiritualism"* blossom!

After an overnight stay with Mary Andrews in the house on Oak Hill Road – referred to as the *"Spiritual Temple"* – Mrs. Lincoln traveled back by train to the National Hotel (*) in Auburn where she consulted the clairvoyant physician, Dr. Hotaling. She gave the doctor *"credit of giving the best diagnosis of her case ever before given,"* according to The *Auburn Daily Bulletin* (2/27/72). *(The article also reported her visit to Moravia to see Mary Andrews.)*

Mrs. Lincoln had always been interested in the supernatural. It was well-known that after the loss of Tad – *the Lincolns' youngest son* – she set up a *'séance room'* in the White house so that she and the President could have a *'medium'* come, on a weekly basis, to conduct *'seances'.*

> *(Throughout history Mary Todd Lincoln has been described as "crazy" ... in fact, Robert – the oldest son – had her committed to an asylum ... because "she believed in spirit world.")*

(*) One hundred years later, Mrs. Lincoln's stay at the hotel was verified by historian, Richard Palmer when he located her signature in the National Hotel register while doing research for an article that would later appear in the March 9, 1975 edition of the Herald American "Empire" magazine. *(On the same page as the article there is a drawing of the hotel that the author of this book did – a drawing done prior to the research being conducted by Mr. Palmer. Needless to say the "discovery" of her signature added to my own research about 'Spiritualism's beginnings in Cayuga County'.)*

In Henry C. Whitney's book, *Life On The Circuit With Lincoln,* he writes about the President's belief in the spirit world. "He communed often with invisible spirits, and talked with a personal God." Whitney also refers to Lincoln as *"a mystic"* in the book..

> *(It is important to note that Mr. Whitney was not only a 'personal friend' of the President but he was the first to write a biography of Lincoln ... shortly after the assassination!)*

History also tells us that President Lincoln "did not go to church" and was often confronted by the media because of his "lack of attendance." *(Not attending church at that time was consider a 'taboo' and so his non-attendance was widely known!)*

There came a time when the President was cornered by the news media and was asked, "What is your belief, Mr. President since you don't go to Church?" And he replied: "If I do good ... then I feel good and if I do bad ... then I feel bad. That, gentlemen, is my religion!" He then walked away.

However, he may have attended church after all! It was reported in the *Buffalo Daily Courier* that after being elected President of the United States and prior to taking office on February 12, 1809, he boarded the train in Illinois and en-route, got off the train in Buffalo where he spent a weekend with Millard Fillmore – *our nation's 13th U.S. President* – who was a known Unitarian. It was because "Unitarians have no creeds or dogmas" that Lincoln decided that he would accompany Fillmore to his church. Therefore, there is the one exception ... he did go to church ... one time!

Certainly Lincoln is also remembered for having been born in log cabin. This is likewise true of President Fillmore. The only other President born in one was James Garfield.)

It may be of importance to mention that the next time that Lincoln and Fillmore were together was after Lincoln's assassination, when his body was being returned to Illinois. Fillmore got on the funeral train in Batavia, New York and rode it to Buffalo, where he got off.

+ + + + + + + + + + + + + + + + + +

MORAVIA AND ITS PAST

In 1966, Leslie L. Luther wrote an exhaustive history of Moravia and environs. In 2007 it was reprinted. Despite the fact that Moravia had a rich history of 'Spiritualism' and was called "The Mecca of Spiritualism", in Luther's book, only 1 ½ pages were dedicated to it. What was included in the book on pgs. 256 and 257 was the following:

"In the period following the Civil War when that doctrine called "Spiritualism" manifested itself, a group of Moravians became disciples.

"One of the earliest here was Mr. Morris Keeler, known to his friends as "Mod"... of a very substantial and respected family. His obituary in the *Moravia Republic* on May 13, 1886, states: "After a lingering illness of many months, Morris Keeler's spirit passed to the world beyond at midnight, May 6, 1886. Mr. Keeler was born in the town of Cortridge, Delaware County, N.Y., on June 25, 1804. He was the oldest son of a family of eight children, four of whom are still living: William, Israel, Mrs. Sally, widow of Henry Alley; and Mrs. Lucina, widow of James Alley, all residing in this town.

"He came to this town with his parents in 1813. He went to Connecticut when twenty years of age, and after working on a farm one year, he entered a comb factory where he was employed for five years. He then returned to this place and bought the farm on which he died, having lived there fifty-five years.

"On June 8, 1830, he was married to Mary Abbott of Danbury, Conn., who survives him. John Keeler, father of Morris, was one of the early settlers in this town, having come here in 1813, living one year in a log house near the place now occupied by E. J. Brown, across the lake, and in 1814 purchasing of John Stoyell for $1,000, fifty acres of the farm on which Morris died.

"Morris Keeler always helped the good of this town, and was one of the leading minds in securing the building of the Southern Central Railroad.

"He was one of the earliest believers in Spiritualism and spent much time and money to its investigation, and the more he investigated the stronger was his belief. About seventeen years since, he built the present dwelling upon his farm, which contained the 'Spiritual Temple', for many years was known throughout the country and Europe. While Mrs. Mary Andrews was there as a Medium, Moravia became the mecca of Spiritualism, and it was no uncommon thing to see twenty-five or thirty strangers at one time who had come to witness the phenomena from a half dozen states, many of them noted as among our greatest thinkers and who had achieved reputations in different professions.

"Mr. and Mrs. Keeler never were blessed with children, and Mrs. Keeler, the only remaining member of the family is in very poor health. Mr. Keeler's funeral was held at the house, Rev. G.H. Bailey (of the Congregational Church) officiating, and a large concourse of people followed the remains to their resting place in Indian Mound Cemetery."

Luther writes that his "mother, as a girl, lived in this Keeler home on Oak Hill for a period and helped Mrs. Keeler, who was blind during her last years. In appreciation Mrs. Keeler gave her a small tilt-top "Spirit Table".

(Luther's mother later donated it to the Cayuga-Owasco Historical Society. It is presently on display at the History House in Moravia.)

Luther writes that his "Mother often told stories of the seances held at this home. Moravia people of the previous generation often recalled the occasion when Mrs. Abraham Lincoln came to Moravia to converse with Abe's spirit."

Luther also wrote an item on March 11, 1866: "A fact that the late Lyman Soule was in faith a Spiritualist, and delighted to witness the mysterious manifestations. Many years ago he owned 'The Cascade', an Inn on the shore of Owasco Lake *(four miles north of Moravia)*, and sold it to a Spiritual *medium*, and meetings were frequently held there. On one occasion the *medium* lost her power and the charm on the magic circle of men and women was broken. Speculation was had as to the cause when Mr. Soule told one of the ladies, 'I know what is the matter, you are sitting cross-legged.' Sure enough, when the woman changed her position the charm was restored and the *spirits* were called into the presence of the living."

Note: The 'fact' that Lincoln's widow came to Moravia and stayed overnight at the home of Mary Andrews is not mentioned by Luther nor does he mention her name in the Index *of his book. One would have had to read the short chapter on 'Spiritualism' to have discovered the fact that* Mary Todd Lincoln came to Moravia, *certainly helping to make Moravia famous by her visit.*

+ +

THE AUBURN 'CIRCLE' – E. W. CAPRON

As already indicated in the first Chapter, the first gathering
of people interested in the phenomenon of *'spirit world'*
occurred in 1849, in the homes of some of Auburn's most
prominent citizens. *(Their names and the homes where the
'circles' were held are listed in that chapter also.)*

It was E. W. Capron – *a well-known author and educator* –
who brought the young girl Catharine Fox to the Auburn
"Circle" on a regular basis. *(She and her younger sister,
Maggie, received national and world-wide attention with the
"rappings" that occurred during their public 'seances'.)*

In his 1855 book *Modern Spiritualism: Facts and
Fanaticisms/Consistencies and Contradictions* … he writes:

"After my investigations in Rochester, I was anxious to
unravel the mystery, if possible, and obtain some rational
solution of what, in the first instance, I was very reluctant to
believe anything of spiritual origin. With a view to satisfy
myself in this respect, I induced the parents of Catharine
Fox, then about twelve years old, to allow her to come to
Auburn, and spend several weeks in our family.

"It was here that we had the best opportunity of seeing and
hearing the manifestations in all their different phases. The
medium was tested in every conceivable way. She slept with
the ladies in the house – different ones – and was tested by
them. No kind of device was left untried to discover if there
could be any trick, or any way of accounting for the strange
occurrences on any known laws, applicable to mundane

phenomena."

After many occurrences took place in the residence, he writes: "it was impossible to conceal the fact that many occurrences were taking place at our residence."

Soon after the first few meetings of the 'Auburn Circle' were held, Capron mentions "the only daily paper printed at the time was the *Auburn Daily Advertiser* that commenced its scurrilous attacks on all who would not shut their eyes and ears to the whole matter."

Capron writes that "it was due to the present editor, Mr. Henry Montgomery writing his false and stupid paragraph that such things awakened inquiry, and had an effect directly opposite to that intended."

Detailed descriptions of what members of 'The Circle' witnessed were provided by Capron. "The manifestations were various and astonishing, consisting of rappings, touchings, moving various articles, and playing on musical instruments."

One incident worth mentioning included a 'common pocket Bible' that "was laid on the table with the strap put through the loop, and awaiting in silence. Soon we would hear the leaves begin to turn and finally we would find the book laying open at some particular chapter, which generally had something to say about *spirits*. Other books have been opened, and appropriate poetry pointed out. The phenomena of pulling the clothing, handling, moving tables, etc., often take place when none present are thinking of them, so that their *wills* do not influence the matter."

Another incident involved a guitar that "was played by unseen hands, and played so exquisitely, too, that it seemed more like far-distant music of an instrument a few feet from us." Capron witnessed the event and names the other credible witnesses to the event at Mr. Bennet's home: "Mrs. Burton Straight, of Troy and R. M. C. Capron, Mrs. G. B. Bennet, H. D. Barron of Auburn."

And at another *circle* "a guitar played by an unseen power to different parts of the room by unseen hands and moved above the heads and was witnessed by James H. Bostwick, Esq., Police Justice, Miss Sarah Bostwick, Mrs. F. Smith, H.D. Barron, and R.M.C. Capron."

Capron relates a number of incidents that occurred during the several *circles* held, naming the witnesses to each. "Two men undertook to hold a chair down, while at their request, a *spirit* moved it, and, notwithstanding they exerted all their strength, the chair could not be held still by them."

At the beginning of Chapter VI, Capron writes: "The number of *mediums* in Auburn, during the summer of 1850, increased very rapidly, until there were from fifty to one hundred in different stages of development."

In that same year the Auburn Circle assumed the title of "The Apostolic Movement."

A Rev. T. L. Harris, of New York City, visited Auburn and he and Mr. Scott "were the external leaders of the movement," They wrote a publication, entitled *"Disclosures from the Interior and Superior Care for Mortals"* that "established their credibility and gave them full control over the whole circle of believers in the Auburn Circle."

Capron writes that "the number of adherents to the cause became quite numerous, several hundreds attending regularly upon the public meetings, and as many as two or three hundred openly identified themselves as supporters of the cause, among whom were some of the most respectable and intelligent people of Auburn ... becoming the largest of any of the religious denominations in the area."

"There was a change of location and the group would need to make what was 'manifested in a dream Mr. Scott had' and the group moved to Mountain Cove, Virginia," according to Capron.

Capron follows the movement to Virginia and witnesses the strife and contention that begins to build. "By February, 1852, several families left the place on account of the contention and want of confidence in the movement."

And, according to Capron, "a few months after a continuation of the discord, the rest left the Cove to the few fanatical and credulous dupes of designing men, until the final dispersion of the whole community a few months after."

Throughout Capron's book his citing of the 'credible' sources are written about in detail. It is in his *Appendix* that the numerous sources who are a part of the on-going controversies which ensued at the time that are worth the telling.

Mentioned earlier is "Catherine Fox's visit to Auburn, in the summer of 1849, the Auburn Daily Advertiser attacked, with

great virulence, all who had anything to do with
investigating the subject."

A small paper, edited by Thurlow W. Brown, called the
Daily Bulletin, occasionally attempted wit on the subject, but
stated they would "make no attempt to impeach the honesty
of persons engaged in the investigation."

The *Rochester Daily News*, edited by John W. Hurn, noticed
the controversy going on in Auburn, and "spoke very fairly
on the subject."

It was the public investigation in Rochester, in November,
1849 at the Corinthian Hall that the public , a full
explanation of the nature and history of the *'mysterious
noises'* supposed to be *'supernatural'* which "have caused so
much excitement in this city and other places for the last two
years," as reported in their local newspaper. Promised was
"an actual demonstration of the sounds, so that they may
know that they are neither made nor controlled by human
beings." It was indicated that "after the lecture, a committee
of five persons chosen by the audience to select any
respectable and convenient room in the city, where the next
day may be devoted to an examination of these
manifestations, and report at the next evening's lecture
whether there is collusion or deception." The public was
invited to, "come and investigate."

The viewpoints of both sides were heard and written about.
One person who responded said, "If only they would look in
the neglected book – the Bible – the mystery would at once
be solved. They would learn that this *spirit,* which seems
principally to be of an associate of certain women, is of the
same character of the *familiar spirits* so frequently spoke of

and condemned in the Bible. The character and works of those, and of this, or these, are similar; near enough alike to be of the same origin – viz., of the devil."

Explained in the New York *Scientific American,* we find the following explanation: *"'Supernatural Knocking. – A knocking at the door* at nights, which has alarmed the good people of Rochester, is explained by Professor Loomis, as "the effect of the vibration of a dam over which the water falls – *they vibrate from the friction of the running water, and the variations depend upon accidental and obvious causes* – producing sounds like a loud knocking on the doors and walls of buildings, and gives a particular account of the phenomenon as observed at the dams of several falls." *(And, he cites them all!).*

In the months of January and February, 1850, a number of articles from the pen of John W. Hurn *(then of Rochester)* were published in the New York *Tribune,* in which he attacked the character of the media, and all persons who had any connection with them. Hurn assumes that "the sounds are electrical and under the control of the *medium."*

It was in the *Northern Christian Advocate*, published in Auburn, N.Y. that "all are assailed who have anything to do with the investigation of the spirit world." The article also questions the credibility of *Mormonism.* "While we repel *Mormonism* in all its phases, and treat with merit contempt the profane mockeries of vulgar impostors, we acknowledge that a candid examination is due to whatever has any just claims to a supernatural character." It is the Northern Christian Advocate's contention that "it is the work of the devil!"

It was the Rev. John M. Austin, a Universalist clergyman of Auburn *(also editor of the Christian Ambassador)*, who puts himself *'on record'* to the matter. He treated the subject very candidly, "presenting a strange contrast to his more orthodox brethren on of the cloth" saying, "many of those who are believers are composed of persons of the various religious sects, and some who sympathize with no denomination. To the extent of my knowledge, they are an intelligent, upright and worthy class of people."

Reverend Austin was the first opponent appearing in the local press who gave the friends of the unpopular truths any credit for honesty!

Capron gives Horace Greeley of the New York *Tribune* credit for giving more space to the discussion of the subject than any other newspaper. "Greeley was one of the best abused men in the country because it was believed he was a full believer, and an 'advocate for the rappers' ... but this is not so!"

Capron carried on a correspondence for up to two years or more with Greeley and says that he "had never known a man, who had the same amount of evidence, to be so far from admitting what I conceive to be their true origin. His accusers were too anxious to make a case against him!"

Among the opposing newspapers, Capron writes "none in the country were more UN-candid than that class known as the religious press, and among these he included the *Boston Investigator.*"

It is the several references that Capron makes of credible individuals who become 'believers' that offer the best arguments.

It is also Judge John Edmonds very lengthy *statement* to the public that is included in Capron's book that deserves to be read by the reader. Capron writes that "Edmonds' whole letter is eminently worthy of preservation, and contains much that should be carefully treasured up by every lover of truth."

(The text of the 'statement' is in the Judge Edmonds' two-volume book series ... a copy of which the author of this book owns. It is a very convincing discourse on the subject and (fortunately) it has since been re-printed and now available on Amazon Books.)

Some of what is included in Capron's book about other credible believers is included in the last chapter of this book … "Voices From The Grave". It is also from "Voices From The Grave" that the play "Circles" *(this author wrote)* was based upon!

Capron writes in his Conclusion: "The foundation on which belief rests is stubborn facts, and no religion ever spread with such unprecedented rapidity, and none has ever rested on such a positive foundation."

A whole century had to pass before it could happen, thanks (again) to world-renowned psychiatrist, Dr. Elizabeth Kubler-Ross's book: "Death and Dying" that credibility has *(at last)* been given to the existence of *'spirit world'!*!

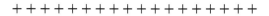

PROPONENTS, RESEARCHERS AND PIONEERS

In the beginning, Horace Greeley, editor of the _New York_ _Tribune_ established a committee to investigate the phenomena and reported the following in his newspaper on June 4, 1850.

> _"We devoted what time we could spare from our duties out of three days to this subject, and it would be the bases cowardice not to say that we are convinced beyond a doubt of their perfect integrity and good faith in the premises. Whatever may be the origin or cause of the 'rappings', the ladies in whose presence they occur do not make them. We tested this thoroughly and to our entire satisfaction."_

News spread across the nation about the Fox sisters who were _"able to communicate with the spirit of a man who had been murdered and buried in their cellar."_ Almost immediately, the girls became famous and their appearances in public places drew large crowds of people. It was a common occurrence for audiences to hear the _'rappings'_ which accompanied the telling of their story.

However, it was because of the cultural and theological shock to the people of the eighteenth and nineteenth centuries that many were not ready to accept _'messages coming from spirit'_ and at more than one point, the Fox sisters were nearly lynched!

In 1855, Eliah W. Capron of Auburn, published in Boston his book, _"Modern Spiritualism"_ which is _(still)_ considered a standard work on the subject. His book tells of some of the *'seances'* which the Fox sisters conducted for some of the most prominent people of the time. One famous gathering included Horace Greeley, William Cullen Bryant, George Ripley, George Bancroft and James Fenimore Cooper.

(Cooper is said to have found the Fox sisters so impressive that he blessed them on his deathbed for having prepared him "for this hour!")

Today's search on amazon.com was successful in that it was discovered that Capron's book has been re-printed.

A few others who are also well worth mentioning include: Joseph Rhodes Buchanan (1814-1899); Judge John Worth Edmonds (1816-1874); Sir Arthur Conan Doyle (1858-1930) and Sir Oliver Lodge (1851-1940). All considered: 'credible'!

Joseph Rhodes Buchanan was a Scientist. He was the Faculty Dean and Professor in the Eclectic Medical Institute in Kentucky. He was involved in pioneer research in *psychometry* and it was he who, in 1842 coined the term *"psychometry"* as meaning the *"measuring of the soul."* In the *Journal of Man,* he published a complete exposition of his system of neurology and anthropology and called this subtle emanation the human body *"aura".* He was one of the very few medical professionals who defended the Fox sisters.

Judge John Worth Edmonds was a member of both branches of the *New York State Legislature* and, for some time, the *President of the Senate* and *Judge of the Supreme Court of New York.* In a letter published in the New York *Herald,* on

August 6, 1853, he wrote: *"I went into the investigation
originally thinking it a deception, and intending to make
public my exposure of it. Having from my researches I have
come to a different conclusion and I feel that the obligation
to make known the result is just as strong. Therefore it is,
mainly, that I give the result to the world. I say mainly
because there is another consideration which influences me,
and that is, the desire to extend to others a knowledge which
I am conscious cannot but make them happier and better."*

Sir Arthur Conan Doyle is probably best remembered for his
'Sherlock Holmes' stories. However, he was both a prolific
writer on the subject of *'Spiritualism'* and an avid proponent.
His introduction to it came while he was a physician during
the years – 1865 to 1888. He firmly associates himself with
the cause of *'Modern Spiritualism'* in his two books: *"The
New Revelation"* and *"The Vital Message."* Both books
were written in his late 1850's, Later, in his two-volume set,
"The History of Spiritualism," he discusses a wide range of
subjects and personalities linked with the Spiritualist
Movement, both in America and the United Kingdom. He
declared his allegiances to *Spiritualism* in 1916 and stated
the following: *"As for the charge of credibility which is
invariably directed by the unreceptive against anyone who
forms a 'position' opinion upon this subject, I can solemnly
aver that in the course of my long career as an investigator,
I cannot recall one single case where it was clearly shown
that I had been mistaken upon any serious point, or had
given a certificate of honesty to a performance which was
after wards clearly proved to be dishonest. A man who is
credulous does not take twenty years of reading and
experiment before he comes to his fixed conclusions."*

Sir Oliver Lodge was a world-renowned physicist. He was also an avid believer in *Spiritualist* concepts. His observations and findings were reported in the *Journal of the Society for Psychical Research (Nov.1884).* He wrote: *"The result of my experience is to convince me that certain phenomena usually considered abnormal do belong to the order of nature, and as a corollary from this, that these phenomena ought to be investigated and recorded by persons and societies interested in natural knowledge."*

Emanuel Swedenborg lived during the reign of Charles XII – from 1688 to 1772. He was an expert in mine engineering, metallurgy, astronomy, physics, zoology, anatomy and political economics. He was best known as an astute Biblical theologian. He also believed that *"the process of death is aided by Angels and that everyone rests for a few days after death and then regains full consciousness on the 'other side'."* He gave the world the *'first catechism'* of Spiritualism!

Andrew Jackson Davis was born at Blooming Grove, a small hamlet along the Hudson River, in New York State. He is often referred to as *"John the Baptist"*of *'Modern Spiritualism'* because in *'trance'* he could always accurately diagnose medical disorders. He was an uneducated man but wrote over 30 books between 1845 to 1885 on subjects from *'cosmological philosophy and dissertation, to health, and a descriptive analysis of the afterlife."* His first book, *"Nature's Divine Revelations,"* went through more than 40 editions. In the later years of his life, Davis acquired a medical degree.

(Books that have since been reprinted and are strongly recommended by this author include: *"Spiritualism"* (Vol. I) by Judge Worth Edmonds and George T. Dexter. Sir Arthur Conan Doyle's books are also well worth reading.)

INSTITUTE OF NOETIC SCIENCES (IONS)

The term noetic sciences was first coined in 1973 when the Institute of Noetic Sciences (IONS) was founded by Apollo 14 astronaut Edgar Mitchell, who two years earlier became the sixth man to walk on the moon. Ironically, it was the trip back home that Mitchell recalls most, during which he felt a profound sense of universal connectedness and what he later described as a samadhi experience. In Mitchell's own words, "The presence of divinity became almost palpable, and I knew that life in the universe was not just an accident based on random processes. . . .the knowledge came to me directly."

Rather than have the reader be told <u>what needs to be told</u> about IONS ... it is suggested that they view a 20-page PDF of the Noetic Post: A 40th Anniversary special edition: http://library.noetic.org/library/publication-newsletters/noetic-post-vol-4-no-1. It celebrates the history of the first 40 years of IONS and the organization's achievements. <u>It covers all anyone would need to know</u>!

<u>THE GOAL OF IONS</u>: "To create a shift in consciousness world-wide ...where people recognize that we are all part of an interconnected whole and are inspired to take action to help humanity and the planet thrive."

THUS … the investigation of "Mediumship"
became one of the areas of focus that the
Institution of Noetic Sciences looked at. A core
group of their scientists and researchers
eventually published a book on the subject and
a new name was given to it: "Channeling" …
which is also the name of book. Thus the
'stamp of approval' was given to it and
'communication with the other side' was
recognized as possible.

Also recognized by IONS as credible is Dr.
Elizabeth Kubler-Ross's materials on 'death
and dying' that are now included in every
nursing program in the United States.

DR. WILLIS W. HARMAN: Scientist, Dr. Harman – who prior to his death in 1997 – was President of the Institute of Noetic Sciences and considered a *'visionary'*. He is remembered for his work with SRI International and also, for raising consciousness within the international business community. Dr. Harman supported the work of Dr. Kubler-Ross. In the 'Noetic Sciences Review' *(Summer 1993)*, he reviews William Baldwin's book, Spirit Releasement Therapy. Throughout, he interjects Baldwin's quotes:
  "When a person dies, it may happen that the spirit remains earthbound for an indeterminate time, *'arrested in the timelessness of the spirit realm, perpetually re-experiencing the mental, emotional, and physical trauma of their death. Just as many human beings are stuck in their birth trauma, so earthbound spirits are often stuck in the death trauma.'* The *earth bound spirit* may be so confused, especially following a violent death, that it does not

recognize that it is dead. It may be so attached to certain elements of its physical life that it '*hangs around*' for another '*fix*'. In general the *earthbound spirit* has lost sight of its purpose – its further evolution as a learning and loving being.

"The clinical evidence suggests that discarnate beings, the spirits of deceased humans, can influence living people by forming an attachment, thus imposing detrimental physical and/or emotional conditions and symptoms. The surviving consciousness of a deceased human becomes a parasite in the mind of the host. It seems to attach itself and merge fully or partially with the subconscious mind of a living person, exerting some degree of influence on thought processes, emotions, behavior, and the physical body.

"An attachment can be benevolent in nature, totally self-serving and malevolent, or completely neutral. Attachment to a particular person can be completely random, perhaps occurring simply because of physical proximity to the dying person at the time of death. In some cases there appears to be a prior relationship, some unfinished business from this or another lifetime. Vulnerability to attachment by a discarnate may result from physical debilitation; altered consciousness through drugs or anesthetics, or unwise experimentation with *channeling*; strong negative emotional state such as rage or terror; or physical or emotional trauma."

Dr. Harman believes there are some similarities between *spirit* attachment and multiple personality disorder. "MPD is almost always a consequence of extreme physical, emotional, or sexual abuse during childhood years … some signs and symptoms of spirit attachment and MPD are similar, so that diagnosis is somewhat of an art … but the goal is fusion, or integration of the alters into the primary personality – or at least cooperation and co-consciousness – the goal of spirit releasement therapy then is to send the lost soul on its way toward further evolution – not *exorcism* or *casting it out* as in some religious traditions, which is likely to leave it seeking some other warm body."

Most of Baldwin's book is descriptions of various cases, illustrating specific points the author wishes to bring out and to convey the flavor, Dr. Harman cites a few of those cases.

There will also be much in the book that the reader will be tempted to reject but the questions is, on what basis do you reject it? Dr. Harman writes, "is it because the experiences related can't be accommodated in a belief system that has served you well up to now?"

Baldwin is "convinced that the great majority of persons have some involvement with *spirit* attachment during some period of their lives, although in most cases they may not be aware of it." Believing in '*spirit* release-ment therapy' he writes, "it is not a substitute for appropriate medical or psychological treatment. It is an approach which takes its place alongside others, for use when the situation calls for it – but not to be ignored because our society has had a taboo against the central concept."

Dr. Willis Harman chose to review the book with the "radical empiricist" credo of William James. "We should insist that our science be based solely in experience, and that it not exclude any experience on the basis of prejudice. Perhaps the spirit attachment hypothesis is only a convenient fiction – a fiction which seems to have helped many patients, and appears to be as benign as believing in Santa Claus. Or perhaps it is a clue to dimensions of reality which our prediction-and-control-focused science has blinded us to. Who can tell?"

+ + + + + + + + + + + + +

Recommended referrals and reading include:

The International Association for Near-Death Studies, at the University of Connecticut, Stores, Connecticut.

Ian Stevenson, *Children Who Remember Previous Lives* (University Press of Virginia, 1987); Arthur Hastings, *With the Tongues of Men and Angels* (Holt, Rinehart and Winston, 1991); Brian Inglis, *Natural and Supernatural: A History of the Paranormal* (Prism Press, 1992; Rosalind Heywood); *Beyond the Reach of Sense* (E.P. Dutton, 1974) and Morris Netherton, *Past Lives Therapy* (William Morrow, 1978)

(This author attended the Sequoia Seminar with Dr. Willis Harman, the weekend of April 30 – May 2, 1993. The retreat center where the 'seminar' was held is located about ten miles north of Santa Cruz, Ca. Dr. Harman explained in a 'layman's understanding' much of what is covered in his book: Global Mind Change. *At that time, the book had just been released. Even by today's standards,* it is still truly a must-read book!

Without a doubt, no book you've ever read will have the needed 'raising of awareness' that this one will have for you!)

+ + + + + + + + + + + + + +

WHY THE CROWS MAY HAVE COME TO AUBURN

It was on January 28, 2003, that because their numbers had grown, Auburn's crow "roost'" ... here in Cayuga County ... was listed on the crows.net website. *(To find it go to their website:* http://www.crows.net/roost1st.html.)

Biologist Michael Westerfield – in charge of the website – calls "the incredible behavior of crows over the past decade ... a dramatic phenomena." *(Westerfield's website includes a map and lists crow roosts throughout North America.)*

Actually the appearance of crows along the top of the wall of Auburn Prison during the late fall of 1974 may have been the first indicator of what was to come to Auburn!

It was while I was doing volunteer work inside Auburn Prison, one of the inmates *– a Native American –* told me, "crows are lining up along the top of the wall at night and their numbers are growing and if their numbers continue to grow, it has a significant meaning to our people."

As Auburnians now know ... their appearance in and around Fort Hill Cemetery has now become an annual event. Auburn is now "a roost"! *(The cemetery is only a few blocks from the prison.)*

What their presence means!
The crow was also considered a *sacred bird* by the ancient Druids. It is "a very special bird" to the Hindus of India as well. *(They believe crows carry the soul from one life to the next.)* Horace mentions the crow as the *prophet* which, "by its cries, foretells rain." Even the Bible references *crows.*

However, to Native Americans, their belief is that their ancestors/guardian spirits can appear to them in the form of animals or birds. They also understand that the crow call also represents "justice".

What occurred on November 3, 1974?

On that date, a group of around 500 American Indians with the American Indian Movement (AIM) took over the Bureau of Indian Affairs building in Washington, D.C. It was the culmination of their *"Trail of Broken Treaties"* walk.

By taking the <u>only</u> copies of the 374 treaties and 16 agreements between the U.S. government and the Native American tribes, the group intended on bringing attention to their issues, including their *"demands for renewed negotiation of treaties, enforcement of treaty rights and improvement in their living standards."* Included among the treaties taken was the first treaty ever signed that affected this entire Finger Lakes area because it was with the Indians of the Six Nations. The signing was held in the Town of Lancaster, Pennsylvania in June 1744, and it was Chief Logan – the "Mingo" – who spoke on behalf of all Iroquois tribes.

In attendance at the first signing was Benjamin Franklin who printed the treaty at his printing office nearby. Early treaties can be found at: http://earlytreaties.unl.edu/treaty.00003.

Later, the Act of 1871 halted the treaty making process and left open "treaties in need of clarification and resolution." *(To-date ... these treaties still remain in limbo!)*

Chief Logan --"The Mingo Chief"

The Chief was known by many tribal names but he was most often referred to as "Shikellamy," and the "Mingo Chief." *(Mingo means: A United People.)*

He was born around the year 1725 and it is because many historians disagree about where he was born that I asked the question of Chief Oren Lyons of the Onondaga Nation.

Chief Oren Lyons is the *faith keeper* of the Turtle Clan, Onondaga Council of Chiefs, Haudenosaunee *(Six Nations Iroquois Confederacy)*.

According to Chief Lyons, "Logan was born at the site of his people's village, along the stream *(Glen Creek)* that empties into Cayuga lake."

There is a large monument adjacent to the site, on the road along Route 90, just outside of the Village of Union Springs heading south. The plaque tells of the destruction of the site in April 1779 by General Sullivan. *(It was President George Washington who ordered "all Indian villages throughout the Finger Lakes be destroyed ... including their stored food"... because Indians had helped the British during the French & Indian War.)*

"Logan is the friend of white men," Thomas Jefferson once said.

Much is written about the attributes of Chief Logan but all that changed when Colonel Cresap – *in cold blood and unprovoked* – massacred all the Cayuga women and children on their trek to Ohio.

It is because Cresap murdered Logan's relations that Logan's famous words, *"Who Is There To Mourn For Logan"* are inscribed on the obelisk in Fort Hill Cemetery.

Chief Logan's monument

The 56-foot-high obelisk monument commemorates Chief Logan. *(It was erected at Auburn's highest point a century ago and from this site all of Auburn and Owasco Lake can be seen.)* However, the famous Chief of the Cayuga Nation is not buried at Fort Hill Cemetery, he is buried in Ohio.

Fort Hill Cemetery is on a *sacred* Indian mound and at the top, *ley lines* intersect. *(Ley lines – known to have existed millennia ago – wrap around our planet and have energetic significance.)* Sacred sites are linked together by the mysterious alignments of these *ley lines* and at the apex where their lines cross, an accumulation of energies exist. *(The circle of stones at Stonehenge in England is probably one of the most well-known sites where ley lines exist.*

Christians later built their great cathedrals in Europe on top of these *sacred* spots and "Christianized" the sites. Their altars are directly over the spots where *ley lines* cross one another.

We now know that the ability of birds and animals to detect the magnetism that emanates from these *ley lines* is what enables them to navigate when migrating and returning.

(This was confirmed in 2014 by the University of Massachusetts.)

Typically crows are known to roost on or near where *ley lines* meet and at Fort Hill Cemetery at least six *ley lines* intersect. *(More about them is covered in the next Chapter.)*

The crows may be signaling their intent

In the early 1980's when the Native American inmates in Auburn Prison first noticed the arrival of the crows lining up along the wall, they came to believe that *"the crows are there because Chief Logan negotiated the first Native American treaty in 1744 and that 'treaty' must be settled first so that it sets a precedence for all the subsequent treaties that are still unresolved by the U.S. government."*

Over the next two decades … there's also been a gradual increase of thousands of crows roosting annually in Lancaster, Pennsylvania where that first treaty was signed. And, according to a *New York Times* article dated 10/26/11, "the crows have come to roost in Tierre Hutte." *(That's where the massacre of Logan's family occurred!)*

If the 'roosting of crows' at each of these locations is tied to Chief Logan's signing of the first treaty, then – according to Native Americans – the "triangle" signifies that *"the crows – their ancestors/guardian spirits – are asking for the 'justice' that is long overdue them."*

.

The Act of 1871 *"left open treaties in need of clarification and resolution."* And, since nearly one hundred and fifty years have passed and there has never been any action taken on any of the treaties that were "left open" … perhaps the dramatic phenomena of the crows may have something to do with 'justice' after all! The crows may also be signaling what the American Indian Movement in 1974 wanted: *"attention on the issues which had been guaranteed by law."*

There has always been controversy over whether the Cayugas or some other tribe constructed the Indian Mound on which Fort Hill Cemetery was built. *(However, North American archaeological research now supports the view that it was built long before the Cayugas and other Iroquois tribes appeared in the Finger Lakes Region.)*

The much earlier Native Americans were referred to as "Alleghans" *(after the Allegheny Mountains)* who inhabited the middle of North America hundreds of years before the arrival of Columbus, and then these 'ancients' vanished.

Native Americans would have only used the *(Fort Hill)* mound for *sacred* purposes. It would have also been where the ten Sachems *(or Senators)* met. They represented themselves as the Grand Council of the Five Nation Confederacy *(aka: The 'Iroquois Confederacy)*. One of the Sachems was Shikellimus, the father of Chief Logan.

Archaeologically, round mounds are one of the many thousand constructions which dot the North American landscape. However, the mound at Fort Hill Cemetery is considered one of only a handful of the more complex mounds in existence in the world!

There are other mounds that are considerably smaller in central New York. In Cayuga County, there is one in the middle of the Village of Elbridge and one just outside of Moravia. *(As a dowser, this author was able to identify two (2) distinct 'ley lines' which intersect at the top of the mound of Moravia's* Indian Mound Cemetery. *Compass coordinates connect one 'ley line' that come from Fort Hill Cemetery.)*

No one is entirely sure how ancient sites might have been used to communicate with the spirits of *dead* ancestors, but the idea is widely accepted by archaeologists, and what little archaeological evidence that does exist, points toward elaborate rituals held at sacred sites presumably to aid the process. Native Americans were also known to practice 'healing' ceremonies where lines intersect.

And so, it's many, many 'thanks' to the Native Americans inside Auburn's prison that stirred up my curiosity enough to explore the possibility of a *paranormal* connection to the crows coming to Auburn and also to 'ley lines'. The inmates were right about the 'significance of the crows' because it helped the author investigate their connection to 'ley lines'!

(I certainly never expected this big of a reward for having done volunteer work in there!)

What I now foresee is that the topic of *ley lines* is bound to gain the attention of the curious, as well as the more serious investigators of science in the not to distant future!

+ + + + + + + + + + + + + + + + + +

FOOTNOTE: In 1851 most of the land occupied by the mound was sold for $1 to a cemetery association. Thus an archaeological treasure of an ancient civilization became a graveyard. The Fort Hill Cemetery was consecrated on July 7, 1852.

Buried there is William Seward, Lincoln's Secretary of State who purchased Alaska, and Captain Myles W. Keogh, who died with Custer's ill fated U.S. 7th Cavalry in an attack on Sioux Indians.

PARANORMAL EVENTS ON 'LEY LINES'
('ley' is Saxony for 'fire')

The Native Americans believe that when the energy lines run north/south (follows the red road, north to south – or vice versa), there will be peace. When the energy lines run east/west – or vice versa), there will be turmoil. (And indeed … turmoil does now exist … President Trump is in the White House!)

Discovered by Alfred Watkins

The first person in the modern West to identify the existence of "ley lines" – *a term he coined* – was Alfred Watkins, a British amateur antiquarian. In 1921 he discovered that many ancient archeological sites appeared to be arranged along a network of straight lines. He also believed that ancient trading routes followed them.

A decade later, occultist Dione Fortune's novel *"The Goat-Foot God"* described *ley lines* as "Lines of Power that are known only to Witches *(who were not portrayed particularly sympathetically)* who had handed the knowledge of them down from Megalithic times." *Ley lines* were thereafter thought of as being 'energetic and magical' in nature.

Interest in *ley lines* remained high until the beginning of World War II and then, the interest waned. It revived again in the 1960s.

It was also in the '60s that *ley lines* were equated with the Dragon Lines of Chinese Feng Shui, and perceived as energetic meridians linking vortices of earth energy. *(The Chinese have been aware of 'ley lines' for centuries!)*

According to Watkins, "a vortex is the point where two or more ley lines meet that the site of an energy vortex occurs. There exists thousands of such vortices, just as the body has thousands of minor chakras. And just as the body has a few highly developed major chakras, some of the earth's vortices are much more developed than others. Ley lines have the same connection to the earth's vortices that meridians have to the body's chakras."

However, it wasn't until John Mitchell's *The View Over Atlantis* published in 1969 that the modern understanding of *ley lines* truly began to take shape.

It is through dowsing that *ley lines* are located today. *(This writer learned her dowsing skills from Lobo Wolf ... a shaman that I trained with in the late 1970s.)*

Archaeologically, mounds are one of many thousand such constructions which dot the North American landscape.

Most mounds are located in the Mississippi, Ohio and Missouri valleys. There are over 5,000 mounds in Ohio and in Michigan and Wisconsin there exist in excess of 10,000. The mound at Fort Hill is considered one of the very few more complex mounds.

There are also others that are considerably smaller in a few other areas of New York. As stated in the previous chapter, in our own county there is a small one in the middle of the Village of Elbridge and one just outside of Moravia. Another small one is east of Auburn, in the Village of Cazenovia.

44   POSSIBILITIES

Given the fact that the Finger Lakes are the largest 'spring-fed' lakes in the world and possess numerous underground freshwater springs throughout the area, Native Americans believe that ley lines most certainly exist in abundance here!

The uniqueness about *'mounds'* is that they are on *ley lines.* They are part of the Earth's energy system and are also referred to as *'earth-energy lines'.* The mysteries surrounding *'ley-lines'* have puzzled mankind for centuries.

The most intriguing theory for the origin of mound building places is in central America with the Mayan civilization. Either by direct migration, or indirectly by the diffusion of culture, ritual and technology, the Mayan practice of building temple mounds spread into North America along the Gulf Coast and up the Mississippi, Missouri, Illinois and Ohio valleys.

In more recent years, a renewed interest in them has been taking place, especially among the scientific community. The geophysical anomalies that are registered by devices today prove their existence. *(Such a device was used by the University of Massachusetts in their efforts to confirm the existence of mounds ...which in 2015 they were able to do.)*

We now know that these *ley lines* en-wrap our planet and were known millennia ago by the *Ancients.* They recognized that along these *ley lines* there was *'energetic significance'.* Sacred sites are linked together by the mysterious alignments of *ley lines* and at the apex where their lines cross, some form of *accumulation of the energies* exists. Standing stones/circles were erected to mark some of these sacred sites. *(The circle of stones at Stonehenge in England is probably one of the most well known.)*

No one is entirely sure how ancient sites were used but there is wide acceptance by archaeologists that communicating with the spirits of dead ancestors may have occurred.

Other archaeological evidence has been found that points toward other elaborate rituals being held at the *sacred* sites, usually occurring when there was a change in the seasons.

When the Christians came along, cathedrals in Europe were known to have been built at *sacred* spots by early Masons who were also the only stone cutters. (They wanted to guard their trade secret of having built them on *ley lines.*) Altars were erected directly over the spot where *ley lines* crossed. *(It is beneath the floors of cathedrals that most members of royal families were also buried.)*

The sighting of *fairies, spirits, ghosts or even extra-terrestrials* along *ley lines* has been claimed time and time again by people of such prominence as Sir Arthur Conan Doyle of 'Sherlock Holmes' fame. *(He indicates his belief in this in his book: "The Coming of the Fairies")*

Ley lines are generally accepted as being straight, however, there are a number of earth-energy lines that are not straight. It is possible to find the length of a ley line to be twenty to thirty miles, although there is a strong suspicion that length can vary from only a few feet to thousands of miles. The width of a *ley line* varies but the average is 5-1/2 feet and that is the width of the Roman road and it was on *ley lines* that they built many of their roads.

Ley lines often follow fault lines and mountain chains.

Earthquakes often occur along them.

As indicated on page 44, as well as in the previous chapter, it has been recently confirmed by the University of Massachusetts that the ability of birds and animals to detect the magnetism that emanates from these *ley lines* is what enables them to navigate when migrating and returning.

We now know that crows typically roost only where *ley lines* intersect. *(No wonder they came to roost at Fort Hill Cemetery; obviously it's because of the number of ley-lines that intersect there!)*

Anyone who sits or lies over a *ley line* for an extended time will – if they are able to maintain an *alpha state* – sense the energy flow. This can work to advantage in healing or in situations where extra energy is helpful.

The following is taken from the Wikipedia web-site:

"For decades there was a considerable amount of interest by British archeologists and anthropologists 'partly because there were so many *ley lines*,' and the earliest were the Mound Builders. They were the indigenous peoples of North America who, during a 5,000-year period, constructed various styles of earthen mounds for religious and ceremonial, burial, and elite residential purposes ... dating from roughly 3500 BCE to the 16th century CE, and living in regions of the Great Lakes.

"Ley lines are supposed alignments of numerous places of historical interest, such as ancient monuments and megaliths, natural ridge-tops and water-fords."

That phrase was coined in 1921 by the amateur Archaeologist Alfred Watkins, in his books *Early British Trackways* and *The Old Straight Track*. He sought to identify ancient trackways in the British landscape. Watkins later developed theories that "these alignments were created for ease of overland trekking by line-of-sight *navigation* during *neolithic* times, and had persisted in the landscape over millennia."

"In a book called *The View Over Atlantis* (1969), the writer John Mitchell revived the term *ley lines,* associating it with *spiritual* and *mystical* theories about alignments of land forms, drawing on the Chinese concept of *feng shui.* He believed that a mystical network of ley lines existed across Britain."

Today, *ley lines* have been adopted by New Age occultists as sources of power or energy, attracting not only curious New Agers but also locals with their dowsing rods.

There are a number of sites on the earth which emanate a special *"energy"* that exists because of the *ley lines.*

They include: The Circle of Stones at Stonehenge, Macchu Pichu in Mexico, both The Parthenon and The Acropolis in Greece, The Great Pyramid at Giza, The Ayers Rock in Australia, The Nazca in Peru, Arizona's 'Sedona', The Mutiny Bay and also, all the great cathedrals in Europe are built on them.

(The altars in the great cathedrals are located where the lines intersect and where it is said that "a concentration of energy is sensed.")

Ley lines also had great importance to many of our 'founding fathers' who were Masons. They included George Washington, along with 13 other presidents. Another Mason was Benjamin Franklin who published a book about *'Free-masonry'* on his own printing press.

Nine signers of the Declaration of Independence were Free-masons, including the man with the biggest signature: John Hancock.

It was George Washington who laid the cornerstone for the United States Capitol building. Other cornerstones that were laid by Freemasons included both the Washington Monument and the White House.

(Each of the three structures are in alignment with the other and can be easily seen in photographs. All three structures are on the prominent Temporal Anchor ley line which is the same one that runs to Washington, D.C. from the mound in Auburn ... at Fort Hill Cemetery.)

It is also because of the importance of the Mason symbols that appear on our money, etc. that the reader may want to know more about their importance. The Discovery Channel did a comprehensive coverage on "The Secret History of the Masons"_"... it is suggested that the reader check out the http site that follows:

www.nbcnews.com/id/33280724/ns/dateline_nbc-newsmakers/t/secrets-lost-symbol#.WMCYbfLIHGs.

+ + + + + + + + + + + +

Another excellent source of the history of Masons is Dan Brown's book, "The Lost Symbol." His popular and engaging book shines considerable light into the shadows of Freemasonry. Brown paints a rather simplistic picture of the Masons. He portrays them "as 'spiritual seekers' in search of higher truths and greater achievements for all humanity." In his novel, one evil man attempts to ruin all of the lofty secret achievements of this noble group. Yet other evidence suggests a much less black-and-white interpretation of the secret society is known as: The Masons.

The existence of the hundreds of thousands of *'mounds'* in North America *(over 10,000 of them in the Great Lakes Region alone!)* can not be ignored!

> *The author of this book was fortunate to have been trained in 'dowsing' in the mid-1970s by 'Lobo Wolf' ... a Native American 'shaman'.*

This writer has *'dowsed'* at the Fort Hill Cemetery mound and determined where the *ley lines* are and exactly where they flow throughout Cayuga County. Of interest is that along them there has been an occurrence of numerous unusual events, including many events that have important *'historical'* significance!

Auburn's prison has one of the wider *ley lines* going through it and this writer first wrote a feature article about them in the *"Ghosts of the Big House"* which appeared in the local newspaper and it can be found at their site: auburn*/news/ghosts.of.the.big.house/article*. *(The article is also reprinted in its entirety in Chapter VI of this book.)*

The article relates the inmates' stories of the *'paranormal events'* they've witnessed while being incarcerated there. *(I have also witnessed phenomena occur while doing workshops in there, as well as during visits with inmates.)*

Other local mounds

As indicated previously, there are three very small *'mounds'* near Auburn – one that is 17 miles south in Moravia, and another one in Elbridge ... which is a dozen miles northeast of the city. The only other known one in New York State is east of Cayuga County, in Cazenovia, 45 miles east of Auburn.

Places to look
As already mentioned previously, it is in Sir Arthur Conan Doyle's book: *"The Coming of the Fairies"* that he shares his own belief in the existence of 'fairies' … as do many of the Irish folk who also believe in them! Their belief is that *"they can only be seen on the ley lines!"* *(The Irish also believe in the existence of leprechauns!)*

With the exception of a *'stand of white birch'* that can only grow on a *ley line,* they are not easily located … unless you've been trained to dowse for them!

Horticulturists have recently discovered that plants placed within a magnetic field grow more than six times faster than in normal conditions. *(Good news for those with a garden!)*

It is this writer's belief that in the near future more about the existence and importance of 'ley lines' will come to the forefront and their amazing mysteries rediscovered!

The 'Theatrical Tour' of Indian Mound Cemetery

The Cayuga-Owasco Lakes Historical Society (COLHS) sponsored a theatrical tour at the Indian Mound Cemetery in Moravia on 9/17/06.

Two musicians – Ron Van Nostrand and Dan Cleveland – performed a medley of songs from the 1800's. What follows is what was stated by both the following day in the local newspaper – *The Auburn Citizen:*

"We were certainly unaware of what might occur by sitting at the apex of the mound but we later shared with one another what we had both experienced while performing our music ... the sensing of an energizing force and also seeing a glowing green light flow through and around our bodies."

As a *dowser,* I was able to identify two distinct *ley lines* which intersect at the top of the mound in Moravia. One of the compass coordinates connects to one that comes from Fort Hill Cemetery. Another site dowsed confirms a *ley line* from Fort Hill Cemetery to the site where Chief Logan was born.

Also of Historical Interest

Thomas Jefferson's European-style excavation of a mound near his home brought the *'mound builders'* to the forefront in the late 18th century. Jefferson described his effort in his 1783 book, *"Notes on the State of Virginia".*

Samuel Haven published *"Archeology of the United States"* in 1856. He brought into question most of the common beliefs about the *'Mound Builders'.* He, as well as other archaeologists, began to understand America's first great civilization; however, with the start of The Civil War the *"Golden Age of Mound Builders"* ended.

The Historic Sites Act of 1935

The importance of the 'mounds' was the reason that the Historic Sites Act of 1935 was passed. The Act decreed 'Presidential authority' to establish National Monuments and required permits to be approved before archeological investigations could be undertaken on federal land.

The Act also *"provided for the preservation of historic American sites, buildings, objects and antiquities of national significance."*

Due to the recent work done at the University of Massachusetts, the existence of *ley lines* has found further acceptance. 'Findings' confirm that "migratory birds and sea turtles have the ability to sense the Earth's magnetic field." *(Of course, this is crucial to navigating the long-distance voyages these animals undertake during migration.)* Their 'report' can be found in a June 2011 publication: *Nature Communications.*

Geologists have recently found that before a natural disaster such as an earthquake, *ley lines* can become 3 to 5 times wider, which seems to warn animals that a natural catastrophe is impending. Their widths vary … from inches to yards wide!

According to *Wikipedia* there are several major areas of interpretation of alignments:

- *Archaeological:* A new area of archaeological study, archaeogeodesy, examines geodesy as practiced in prehistoric time, and as evidenced by archaeological remains. One major aspect of modern geodesy is surveying.

- *Cultural:* Many cultures use straight lines across the landscape. Straight lines connect ancient pyramids in Mexico. If it was necessary, stairs were cut into sandstone cliffs to facilitate keeping roads straight.

- *New Age:* Some writers widely regarded as pseudo scientific have claimed that the *ley lines* and their intersection points resonate a special psychic or magical energy. These theories often include elements such as geomancy, dowsing or UFOs.

One of the best websites I've found to explain Ancient Ley Line Wisdom can be found at the following site: http: //www.ancientwisdom.com/leylines.htm. On it are the names of the many who have researched them. Anyone curious to know more about them should check the site out.

Natural and a Synthetic Vortex or Ley Line Difference

A synthetic *Vortex* can also occur. It happens when the presence of a large number of people continually moving along a specific road, creating a *ley line* even though the road was not originally constructed upon a ley line. An example of this is when an extremely traumatic experience such the Cherokee Trail of Tears occurred and the route now has the properties of a *Yin ley line*.

Not only the Earth, but the air and the waters have *ley lines* and are very curvilinear in form. *Ley lines* and *vortices* are also found in all parts of space and time. Outer space has *ley lines*, and Earth's *ley lines* serve to connect and integrate with space. The *ley lines* in space are both straight *(Yang)* and curvilinear *(Yin)* like those on the Earth.

Working with *ley lines*

Finding energy *Vortices* may be useful for psychic development. *(Native Americans used them for their ritual ceremonies.)* They typically set up their settlements on *ley lines*.

Living or working on top – or at the intersection – of several *Yang ley lines* can sometimes affect health because of the effect of continual high energy on the body's system. Living or working on a *Yin ley line* can also cause sluggishness and inertia, or it can contribute to disturbing psychic phenomena. *Yin ley lines* can cause the retention of emotional energies, especially traumas, or even hauntings!

The extent of these phenomena in either case depends upon the strength and character of the individual *ley line* in question. By locating the *ley line* … one can determine in advance if a location may be unfavorable for habitation, or one can adjust the energies to make a location more favorable.

Vortices

There are over thirty (30) known locations around the earth that have major *vortices* which emit strong energy levels.

In the United States they are located in Chicago, Mt. Shasta, Sadona and the Smokey Mountains. *(It is the writer's personal belief that because of the existing injustices that exist in Chicago at the present time, the level of discontent in that City is such that the Vortice intensifies it expeditiously and the result is the on-going (unexplained) chaos we are witnessing today!)*

NOETIC SCIENCES

The credibility of *ley lines* has been recently acknowledged by Dr. Deen Radin, a Senior Scientist at the Institute of Noetic Sciences (IONS). He is also Adjunct Faculty in the Department of Psychology at Sonoma State University *(Rohnert Park, Ca.)*. He began his academic career after earning a degree in electrical engineering, *magna cum laude* with senior honors in physics, from the University of Massachusetts (Amherst), a masters degree in electrical engineering and a PhD in psychology from the University of Illinois, Champagne-Urbana.

For over a decade, Dr. Radin has worked on advanced telecommunications R&D at AT&T Bell Laboratories and GTE Laboratories. And, for two decades Dr. Radin has also been engaged in 'consciousness' research.

Before joining the research staff at IONS, Dr. Radin held appointments at Princeton University, the University of Edinburgh, the University of Nevada, and three Silicon Valley 'think-tanks', including SRI International, where he worked on a classified program investigating psychic phenomena for the United States government.

Dr. Radin has presented over a hundred invited lectures in venues including Cambridge, Harvard, Stanford and Princeton Universities, Google headquarters, DARPA, and the United States Navy.

Honey bees & ley lines

Perhaps what may be of interest to the reader is what I found on David Cushman's website *(dave-cushman.net /bee/leylines.httm)*. He believes that he has found a linking of honey bees to *ley lines*!

Cusman is an engineer and was turned on by the work of 'bee navigation and communication' done by Karl von Frisch and wanted to investigate it further. He says that "for an insect to be told by another insect how to visit a food source a mile or more away and return with pinpoint accuracy is incredible."

He was also curious about a theory held by John Harding who said that "all the naturally grown oak trees he ever checked were on 2 or more *ley lines*, many on 4-5 and that many wild honey bee colonies nest in cavities in oak trees."

Cusman believed that "*ley lines* and other markers are likely to be fixed, but the sun – that is central to the discoveries of von Frisch – is constantly moving." He in no way was trying to discredit von Frisch's work, merely suggesting something else may be enhancing it. He'd only ever seen two drone assemblies. "The one in July 2013 was over so many *ley lines* it was impossible for me to count them all. Could it be that both drones and queens follow *ley lines* to the assemblies?"

Since 2009. he has checked every place he knew where a swarm had settled and everywhere a wild colony had set up home and they were all on a place where at least two *ley lines* cross … sometimes several more.

In July 2011 he was called out to witness a swarm on the ground. *(He determined that it was where several ley lines crossed!)*

And, in February 2013 he was asked by an ecologist to "look at a wild colony in a tree". When he got there, it was in the branches of a tree that had blown down and the nest was out in the open. He found it was directly over a spot where at least a dozen *ley lines* crossed. It was also only a short distance from houses, where there were many better places to build a nest. He'd seen many honey bee nests that had been built in the open, all of which had a higher number of ley *lines* crossing through them than those in cavities do, suggesting the concentration is like a magnet to them. The least he ever came across was eight (8) and the most ... a dozen, as mentioned above. And, after checking several hundred sites and speaking to numerous beekeepers, he learned that "bees swarm and settle in the same places." He would later place all his bait hives where two or more *ley lines* cross and was very successful in catching swarms.

The Dragon and The Tiger

The Chinese call *ley* lines "Lung Mei" or "Dragon Lines." *Lung Meis* are perceived as being of two types: *Yang lines* represented by the Blue Dragon, and *Yin lines* represented by the White Tiger. The intersection of the two, balancing *Yin and Yang*, is perceived as a power center and that is a vortex. The same duality is perceived in the west also.

Yang ley lines are normally at the surface and just below the surface of the Earth. They are straight lines which form geometric shapes, especially triangles. And, when they cross each other – which they often do – they often emit or give a feeling of high energy that is sometimes described as 'invigorating or electric' … tending to increase physical energy. When they are at their strongest, they can produce an underground effect. This is why when too many *ley lines* intersect in one spot … life can be disruptive!

Yin ley lines are typically deeper in the Earth and are normally associated with underground water – subterranean rivers and springs. *Unlike the straight Yang ley lines, Yin ley lines* are circuitous and curvilinear. *Yin ley lines* "give a feeling of heavy, slow energy sometimes described as calm and peaceful." They can both dampen physical energy but heighten psychic energy and can have an effect on meditative states. It is often difficult to live over a *Yin ley* line because of the passive atmosphere that it creates and which can be very difficult to function on an every day level.

(Buddhists have always been aware that when the two kinds of ley lines intersect, a powerful energy is formed which includes the qualities of both, though not always in equal measure.)

The idea that there are both *Yang and Yin ley lines*, and that both connected with the ancient Megalithic monuments is supported by the early work of dowsers M. Louis Merle and Regional Allender Smith. And, just as Watkins demonstrated a relationship between ancient monuments and straight *ley lines* during the 1920's, it was during the 1930's that Merle and Smith demonstrated a similar relationship between the ancient monuments and the presence of underground water sources and frequently of freshwater springs: that is to say, *Yin Ley Lines.*

+ + + + + + + + + + + + + +

GHOSTS OF THE BIG HOUSE

Inmates will deny their existence, but some have told me – privately – stories about the *ghosts* that share Auburn Prison with them. And, based on what I was told, I believe I have been able to identify a few of them.

Considering the prison in Auburn, New York is 190 years old at the time of this writing, it isn't surprising these restless *spirits* are former residents there. The ones I have identified were electrocuted in the prison with one exception, Rachel Welsh.

The first electrocution in the United States took place here in Auburn on August 6, 1890. William Kemmler was the first victim of the chair *(President William McKinley's assassin)*. Leon Czolgosz was next to be electrocuted in 1901. In total, 55 inmates were electrocuted in Auburn between 1890 and 1916. Only one of them was a woman.

Many who die in prison are unprepared to die and stay "earth bound," and for those who were electrocuted, they usually all remain "earth-bound *spirits*."

Inmates' stories

In 1974, I was asked to coordinate inmate programs for the Auburn Jaycees. The organization had set up the first "Jaycee Chapter" in the prison the previous year. They were able to do this because one of the "28 points" that State Corrections Commissioner Russell G. Oswald agreed to after the Attica 'uprising' was that *"service organizations, churches, agencies, etc. help institute realistic, effective rehabilitation programs for all inmates according to their offense and personal needs."*

Through my involvement with the <u>New York State Council on the Arts</u>, I received a grant to fund an <u>inmate art program</u>. It put me in touch with a select number of gifted inmates who had developed their art skills after coming into prison.

After several weeks of classroom involvement with these prisoners, I approached some about whether they were aware of any *ghosts* in the prison. Many dismissed my question, but a few admitted they believed they existed. A few candidly told me that while they were drawing or painting in their cells, they sensed they were being observed, that they were aware of a "presence." When I asked how often this occurred, their answers were "maybe once." However, two of them told me, it happened several times. One inmate said, "As soon as I turned to look, the *ghost* was gone."

Those who acknowledged "the presence of a *ghost*" also told me, they "were totally convinced it was indeed, a *ghost.*"

Most of the inmates I talked with were housed in C Block. *(This is where most of the 'ghost sightings' seemed to occur. This is also the section of the prison which was originally referred to as 'The North Wing'.)*

These same inmates also told me they sometimes heard "strange sounds" that – they were sure – did not come from any of the other guys on their tier. A few even admitted the sounds were "sometimes frightening."

(The importance of events occurring in C Block has a connection to the "ley line" that passes through it!)

The original North Wing

Gutted after the 1929 *riots,* the original North Wing was completed in 1821 and was made up entirely of solitary cells. These 83 cells were 7-feet long, 7-feet high and 3 1/2-feet wide. The cells were lined up, back to back, and stacked, five tiers high. On Christmas Day 1821, the first group of "worst offenders" were consigned to these cells and kept continually in solitary confinement.

Flogging inmates was legal then in New York State, so these inmates were subjected to it daily. In less than a year, five of the 83 men had died. Many went insane - one even jumped to his death as soon as his door was opened. The results of this experiment so horrified the state, the system was abandoned and most of the survivors were pardoned.

In the early 1800s, thousands of sightseers visited Auburn Prison and paid the price of admission, 12 1/2 cents, to view inmates as they worked in shops. There were narrow passages in the rear of the shops through which they could watch the convicts. To reduce the large numbers of visitors, the fee was doubled, but it did not deter spectators willing to pay the price to peek! *(These passageways still exist today!)*

Is it any wonder why Alcatraz Island has become the number one "tourist attraction" in San Francisco? It is because of the willingness of people to wait in line for hours that tourists now have to make reservations in advance in order to visit the former prison in California.

The women who died inside

One inmate told me because he had good peripheral vision,

he was able to catch a glimpse of a *ghost* standing outside
his cell. "It was definitely a woman from the last century," he
told me. "She came back again, the following night, but I
continued to paint and she continued to watch." It was on
this visit that he was able to get a better description of her
and I wrote down what he said in my notebook.

 Sometime later, when a copy of an old newspaper drawing
of Mary Farmer came into my hands, I recalled the inmate's
description and I was convinced it might be her. *(She'd been
electrocuted in Auburn Prison on May 29, 1909.)* When I
showed the drawing to the inmate, he was sure it was the
same woman who'd stood outside his cell that night.

Another inmate told me he was awakened one night by the
sound of crying. He saw a woman standing inside his cell.
"She was holding a baby in her arms and she was sobbing,"
he said. After a few seconds, the vision before him faded.
He was taking medication at that time and, although
convinced he might have really seen a *ghost*, he told me he
also believed the medication may have caused an illusion.

Nevertheless, he described the woman he saw standing in his
cell and I wrote it down. Later, while I was doing research, I
came across his description. It matched another prominent
woman prisoner - Rachel Welsh. She had arrived at Auburn
Prison in January 1825 and died there Jan. 9, 1826.
However, six weeks prior to her death she gave birth to a
child she'd clearly conceived while in prison. An
investigation ensued as a result of public outcry. Evidence
showed she'd been whipped severely on many occasions.
The commissioners appointed to look into the circumstances
of her pregnancy and death wrote in their report, "The

punishment inflicted upon Rachel Welsh had no connection with her death." *(But there was no mention in the report about how she got pregnant after coming into the prison.)*

Protecting myself

It is important to note, that while I was coming into the prison during the 1970s, I was also training with my spiritual teacher and a *'medium',* the Rev. Mae Merritt York. At her insistence, I made the commitment to 'volunteer' my time in the prison as a way of fulfilling my requirements for the "licentiate" ministry. She also reminded me of what Christ had said about "the need to go into the prisons to help," as recorded in the Bible in Matthew 25, vs. 36 – 39. She said that I *"needed to break down barriers that existed between me and my brothers"* and also, the importance of learning the "truth." After all, I had grown up in Auburn where, because of the prison, there seemed to exist an unhealthy prejudice towards anyone who showed any empathy towards inmates. *(And the same strong bias exists today!)*

As I look back, it is somewhat ironic that the high school I attended was across the street from the front wall of Auburn Prison. And, the house I lived in on South Street was directly across the street from where the warden lived!

Growing up in Auburn, I dismissed the whole prison issue and yet, a quarter century later, I was going to have to face it. And, I knew I would not be comfortable about it. I also knew it would be difficult because I could expect some repercussions from the community.

(Indeed, it was what became a 'wake-up call' for me!)

The relic

A week prior to my going into the prison coincided with meeting a Greek priest visiting the United States for his first time. He was related to a man I had worked for when I was in high school. This priest had escaped from a Nazi prison camp during World War II.

"Pappas" did not speak English but his nephew did. During our conversation, he was told I was planning on going into the prison to work with inmates. The priest excused himself but indicated he'd return and I should wait. When he finally returned, he handed me "a relic." In the ensuing translated conversation I learned of its importance. His instructions were that I *"wear it whenever I went into the prison because of my interest in 'spirits',"* and that I keep it close to me - at all times - because, he said, *"it offered protection against evil spirits and/or entities that might come around me."*

To this day, 40 years later, I still wear it, pinned inside my garment, or have it no more than 10 feet from me.

What is unfortunate is there are so many 'earth-bound *spirits'* inside all the 'big houses' with no opportunity provided so that qualified clergy can go into the prisons to help these *lost souls* transcend the bars that bind them.

+ + + + + + + + + + + + + + + + + +

THE AUBURN PARAPSYCHOLOGY GROUP

According to Wikipedia: *"Parapsychology is a field of study concerned with the investigation of paranormal and psychic phenomena which include telepathy, precognition, clairvoyance, psychokinesis, near-death experiences, reincarnation, apparitional experiences. It is often identified as pseudoscience."*

A history of 'parapsychology' is provided by *Wikipedia* and worth repeating: "For decades the research of parapsychology has been conducted by private institutions in other countries and often funded through private donations. Any findings rarely appeared in mainstream science journals but if there were any papers about parapsychology, they were typically published in a small number of niche journals. The investigation of parapsychology continued for over a century without any convincing evidence and so it was continually criticized.

"The earliest known experiments were conducted in 1858 by chemist Robert Hare who conducted experiments with *mediums* that sometimes proved successful. Several others also conducted experiments on *mediums* and they included Frank Podmore, Agenor de Gasparin and the renowned German astrophysicist Johann Karl Friedrich Zollner.

"In 1882, the Society for Psychical Research was founded in London. It was the first systematic effort to organize scientists and scholars to investigate paranormal phenomena. Early membership included: Henry Sidgwick, Arthur Balfour, William Crookes, Rufus Osgood Mason and Nobel Laureate Charles Richet. Their areas of study included telepathy, hypnotism, Reichenbach's phenomena, apparitions, hauntings, and the physical aspects of *Spiritualism* that included table-tilting (*), materialization and apportation.

"In 1911, Stanford was the first academic institution in the United States to study extrasensory perception (ESP) and psychokinesis (PK). The effort was headed by psychologist John Edgar Coover.

"In 1930, Duke University became the second major U.S. academic institution to engage in a critical study of ESP and psychokinesis in the laboratory. Psychologist William McDougall headed the effort, with the assistance of psychologists, Louisa and Joseph Rhine and Karl Zener. Their volunteer subjects were from the undergraduate student body. A quantitative, statistical approach was used. Using cards and dice, they were successful. Despite much criticism from academics and others who challenged the concepts and evidence of ESP, their procedures for the testing of ESP came to be adopted by interested researchers throughout the world."

Parapsychological Association

It was on June 19, 1956 that the formation of the Parapsychological Association (PA) was proposed by J.B. Rhine at a workshop which was held at the Parapsychology Laboratory at Duke University. The aim of the organization, as stated in its Constitution, was "to advance parapsychology as a science, to disseminate knowledge of the field, and to integrate the findings with those of other branches of science".

In 1969, under the direction of anthropologist Margaret

Mead, the Parapsychological Association (PA) became affiliated with the American Association for the Advancement of Science (AAAS), the largest general scientific society in the world. The affiliation of the Parapsychological Association (PA) with the American Association for the Advancement of Science, led to a decade of increased parapsychological research.

Other organizations were also formed, including the Academy of Parapsychology and Medicine (1970), the Institute of Parascience (1971), the Academy of Religion and Psychical Research, the Institute of Noetic Sciences (1973), the International Kirlian Research Association (1975), and the Princeton Engineering Anomalies Research Laboratory (1979).

Two universities that still have academic parapsychology laboratories include the University of Virginia's Department of Psychiatric Medicine. *(Their work includes "the survival of consciousness after bodily death, near-death experiences, and out-of-body experiences.")* The University of Arizona's *Veritas Laboratory* conducts laboratory investigations of *mediums.*

The above universities, as well as several other private institutions – *including the Institute of Noetic Sciences* – conduct and promote parapsychological research. A result of their combined research on mediumship has been confirmed and they now call it: *"channeling".*

Parapsychology research is currently represented in some 30 different countries and a number of universities worldwide continue academic parapsychology programs.

Today's research and professional organizations include the following: the Parapsychological Association; the Society for Psychical Research, publisher of the *Journal of Society for Psychical Research;* the American Society for Psychical Research, publisher of the *Journal of the American Society for Psychical Research;* the Rhine Research Center and Institute for Parapsychology, publisher of the *Journal of Parapsychology;* the Parapsychology Foundation, which periodically publishes the *International Journal of Parapsychology;* and the Australian Institute of Parapsychological Research, publisher of the *Australian Journal of Parapsychology.*

Parapsychological research also incorporates other sub-disciplines of psychology which includes transpersonal psychology which studies transcendent or spiritual aspects of the human mind, and anomalistic psychology, which examines paranormal beliefs and subjective anomalous experiences in traditional psychological terms.

THE AUBURN PARAPSYCHOLOGY GROUP

In 1971, a group of interested professionals responded to an ad the author put in the local newspaper. They named themselves *"The Auburn Parapsychology Group".* They recognized their interest in *'parapsychology'* and so they "began the process of learning more about an upsurge at the time in the expansion of consciousness."

They agreed that the first step was to begin the arduous reading of books on the subject and so, over the course of the next two years, every available book on related topics were read. A majority of the books were deemed "'unfit"!

The books read were singled according to topics which more closely related to their own area of expertise. For example, the person with a master's degree in botany read books on the healing effects of herbs. The engineer with a background in mathematics read books on astrology. The psychologist read books on extra sensory perception (ESP), etcetera.

Eventually a 'recommended reading list' of nearly 100 books was agreed upon which the group believed "best represented the new field of parapsychology." Those books were then donated to the Seymour Library. *(A year later, Steve Erskine, the library's director, told the group that "the donated books were the library's most checked out in the decade that followed.")*

In 1973, the YMCA's program director, Mary Kelly gave the group the 'go ahead' and do a ten (10) week series on parapsychology. *(Over 50 people signed up for the series and all proceeds were donated to the "Y".)* A second year's series was also done for the 'Y' and again, a big sign up! And, although members of the Auburn Parapsychology Group were *'speakers'* of the YMCA workshops, there were also *'guest speakers'* that included: Dr. Lila K. Piper, Dr. Peter Guy Manners and Dr. Edgar Mitchel. *(All three are now deceased.)*

DR. LILA PIPER *(sociology) – Graphologist*

Graphology is the analysis of the physical characteristics and patterns of handwriting purporting to be able to identify the writer, indicating their psychological state at the time of writing, or evaluating personality characteristics employment profiling.

Dr. Piper was a former Dean of Women at Syracuse University. *(Her husband, Dr. Raymond F. Piper was Professor Emeritus of Philosophy at Syracuse University.)*

She was often approached by major companies/businesses to evaluate the hand-writing 'sample' of an applicant. She was able to do a personality profile, matching the congruency of the applicant with the ideal psychological profile of employees in the position being interviewed for.

I was fortunate to know this remarkable woman and twice visited her in her home in Skaneateles. She gave me a copy of a book that she and her husband co-authored, entitled: "Cosmic Art" that was published in 1975 with the forward written by Ingo Swann.

That same year, she came to my home and met with several professionals who'd graduated from Syracuse University but who had also attended her husband's philosophy classes back in the late 50's. *(They came to witness their own hand-writing being analyzed.)* One of those who attended was a psychiatrist who admitted he was "astonished by the accuracy of the analysis" he'd been given.

A year later, when I asked if she'd do a workshop inside Auburn prison her response was, "of course!" *(Of the several workshops that were offered to inmates, hers was 'their favorite!')*

It is worth mentioning that although there was a back-gate entrance into the prison that would have been a short distance to the school where the workshops were being conducted, the administration *(in an effort to discourage her)* informed Dr. Piper – a woman in her early 80's – that "to get to the school, she would have to walk the entire length of the yard that was full of inmates." Her response … "I expected that!"

Although there continues to remain skepticism about the credibility of 'graphoanalysis' ... her ability was certainly convincing to all those who had their handwriting analyzed.

Today's young people have no exposure to learning how to write ... some do learn how to print ... but the handwriting of most is not at all legible! *(Therefore there really is no further need to know how to analyze one's handwriting is there?).* Still, I'm thankful that I learned the *'Palmer Method'* of handwriting.

DR. PETER GUY MANNERS, M.D., PhD *(physics)* **L.B.C.P., F.I.C.T.M., D.D. M.H. M.A.**

Dr. Manners was a pioneer in sound therapy. He was also a British osteopath, qualified in England and Germany, specializing in natural and electromagnetic medicines.

Dr. Manners studied and collaborated with many outstanding scientists, including Dr. Hans Jenny *(Switzerland)* and Dr. Harold Saxon Burr of Yale University *(U.S.).* He researched the use of cymatics and biomagnetics for medical diagnosis and treatment, including the healing effects of certain sound vibrations and harmonics on the structure and chemistry of the human body, as well as the importance of sound and light in our natural environment.

Prior to his demise, he ran the Brentforton Scientific and Medical Trust at the Bretforton Hall in Vale of Evesham, Worcester, England. Although I visited him there in 1980, it was in 1975 that I first met him when he did a workshop on *"Colors' Effects on Healing"* at Cayuga Community College.

After his talk before students and faculty, he met privately with members of the Auburn Parapsychology Group and showed us the first *'Kirlian'* photography we'd ever seen! *(Seeing color auras around individuals that confirmed human conditions was a first for all in attendance!)*

He talked to us about his work which he called: "Cymatics … the application of certain sound frequencies directed at acupuncture points as a way of promoting healing." *(When I told him after talking to the group that I wanted to know more about it, I was surprised by his answer, "One day you'll visit me in Evesham and I'll get you involved in it"... and he walked away.)* At the time, his answer made no sense to me at all … and I dismissed it!

But then in 1980, my friend Alice Greene called me and said that she and her husband "were planning to make a trip to England to see Dr. Manners" and would I "like to come with them as their guest?" Of course I said, "yes!"

THE TRIP TO ENGLAND & WALES

I will write a great deal more about my trip to England in the Chapter – **REINCARNATION** – and therefore no need to do so at this time. *(The trip's importance to 'reincarnation' is why it's being brought up in that chapter!)* But there is more about what needs to be said here about the meeting with Dr. Peter Guy Manners at his Clinic at Vale of Evesham, Worcestershire … just outside of London.
What will be indicated in that Chapter is that I accompanied Dr. Manners to his office and he tells me the details of what I had experienced the previous day, etcetera.

It was because he told me he knew I was "a clairvoyant" and that he "had psychic abilities also" that he asked me if I "recalled his telling me back in Auburn" that I'd "come to England one day and would learn more about Cymatics at that time?" And I said, Yes, I did remember!" And, of course I was still very interested in knowing more about it and said so. He said that my "being a cymatics technician would help in the development of becoming a 'healer'."

He reminded me that "whenever we're healed, the healing convinces oneself that healing is made possible through a higher power and that it can come through the *healer's* hands ... thus we can become the *channels* for healing."

And so, after the completion of my training with Dr. Manners, both in England and later in Boston, when he came again to the U.S. to teach and to lecture, I became a *Cymatic Technician* and was able to be registered with the *National Association of Healers*.

Dr. Manners was a believer in Karma. This became obvious to me because of what he later told me. *"There is an important reason why you and Jim are together in this lifetime and a part of the reason is the need to forgive him for what he did in that lifetime."* (He inferred that it was I who had been his 'victim' in that previous lifetime!)

CYMATIC APPLICATOR

The Cymatic Applicator is shaped like a phone with out the mouthpiece and is connected by a cord to a box that contains the micro-circuit that generates the frequencies.

Dr. Manners gave *'lungs'* as an example, saying that "research has shown that whatever the frequency of 'healthy' lungs is, the way to restore the 'unhealthy' tissue to a 'healthy' state is to administer the specific frequencies that has been determined for a 'healthy' lung." *(The frequencies that research had established were done by measuring the natural resonant frequency of the many tissues in a healthy body. The frequencies had been measured in both the healthy and previously diseased state.)*

Although the frequency 'process' may be used for any blockage in the body - tumor, calcification, or internal bruising for example - the applicator may also be used for viral infections, bacteria and diseases of the blood.

Later I recorded all of the Cymatic frequencies onto cassette tapes. When I told Dr. Manner what I had done and that I was able to get the same result by having the patient hear the frequency, he responded, "of course that'll also work. It's the brain syntax that will recognize it as the 'correct frequency' and jump-start the healing process."

Dr. Manners wrote several booklets and I have them all. Topics include: *Music Therapy, Aspects of the Healing Spectrum, Cosmic Influences on Human Behavior, Another Way & Another Direction, Cymatics and Its Integrating Phenomena, Cymatics in Relation to the Meridian System, Press Information, The Spirit of Medicine: Uniting Science and Art, Effects of Electromagnetic and Cymatic Energy on the Nervous System, The Emergence of New Age Medicine, Healing and Regeneration through Music, A Wave of the Future and Homeopathy.*

TODAY'S PRACTITIONERS
Today's practitioners call it: **Cyma** … "a proprietary form of cymatic (or sound) therapy." It is being practiced worldwide by medical doctors, osteopaths, acupuncturists, message therapists, chiropractors, and other complementary practitioners and it's become BIG BUSINESS.

(A search on "Cyma Therapy" produced names of hundreds of practitioners in the United States and within a 100 mile radius ... there were three (3) practitioners found!)

DR. EDGAR MITCHELL *(astronaut)*

At the Cayuga Community College workshop in 1975, Dr. Mitchell talked about his recently formed Institute of Noetic Sciences (IONS) organization.

On their website – noetic.org it says: *"The term noetic sciences was first coined in 1973 when the Institute of Noetic Sciences (IONS) was founded by Apollo 14 astronaut Edgar Mitchell, who two years earlier became the sixth man to walk on the moon."*

Ironically, it was on the trip back home that Mitchell says he recalls most, *"it was during the return trip that a profound sense of universal connectedness was experienced. The presence of divinity became almost palpable, and I knew that life in the universe was not just an accident based on random processes. . . .The knowledge came to me directly."* (He later described it as a *samadhi experience.*)

Trained as an engineer and scientist, Dr. Mitchell shared his experience with those of us who attended his workshop. He talked about his walking on the moon … *"an experience for which nothing in life had prepared him for."*

As he approached the planet he knew as home, he said he *"was filled with an inner conviction as certain as any mathematical equation he'd ever solved."* Saying also that *"the beautiful blue world to which he was returning is part of a living system, harmonious and whole – and that we all participate in this universe of consciousness."*

Captain Mitchell said he *"was most comfortable in the world of rationality and physical precision and the understanding that came to him as he journeyed back from space represented another way of knowing what is that truth."*

This experience apparently altered his worldview! Despite science's superb technological achievements, he realized that we have "barely begun to probe the deepest mystery of the universe – the fact of consciousness itself." He said he "became convinced that the uncharted territory of the human mind was the next frontier to explore, and that it contains possibilities we had hardly begun to imagine." Within two years of his expedition, Edgar Mitchell founded the Institute of Noetic Sciences (INS) in 1973."

On the *noetic science website* Mitchell's conclusion is noted: *"Perhaps a deeper understanding of consciousness (inner space) could lead to a new and expanded understanding of reality in which objective and – outer and inner – are understood as co-equal aspects of the miracle of being."*

How fortunate that Dr. Mitchell's efforts to launch the interdisciplinary field of noetic sciences happened during this period of time.

The writer of this book was also fortunate to attend several of the annual conferences conducted by IONS in the Bay Area during 1990s and heard Dr. Mitchell and many others speak about their work.

Having met him personally was another one of those rare but *'fortunate'* blessings in my lifetime … helping me to know that I am not alone in my belief that there is no death but that we do transcend!

PARAPSYCHOLOGY WORKSHOPS CONTINUE

As indicated above, the group was later granted permission to bring their 'series' into the Auburn Correctional Facility to inmates that were members of the Logan Jaycee Chapter.

In the fall of 1990, the Cayuga Community College offered a 'sampling' of five alternative approaches to wellness. Their brochure read: "for anyone who wanted to find out more about the growing field of alternative medicine." *(I was able to participate as a 'speaker' and also able to enlist the other four (4) 'speakers' for the series.)*

In 2005, the Auburn Parapsychology Group was again asked to provide speakers for another series of workshops at the local college. They included:

(1) Dr. Michael, a psychiatrist in Ithaca, explained why he "no longer used prescription medicine but homeopathy remedies instead."
(2) Dr. John Chang, a chief orthopedic surgeon in China prior to coming to the United States, spoke about acupuncture and did a demonstration on those in the class who were willing to having it done on them.
(3) The writer of this book who talked about *Cymatics* and also *Color Therapy ... "the healing effects of color and sound on the body".*

Our group's first participation at the local community college opened the door to more 'alternatives' being offered and since the 1990's there are now classes/workshops in: Feng Shui, Yoga, Qigong, Judo, Kung Fu and Reiki.

Since the early 1990s the acceptance of 'alternatives' is also evident in many of today's TV shows, including the popular weekday "Dr. Oz" show. He is not only "a believer of many alternatives" but he is also a major supporter of "bringing 'alternatives' into the field of wellness."

A recent trip to the local library finds many of those donated books missing from the bookshelves … no doubt either not returned or intentionally removed by *(perhaps)* a closed-minded Christian!

+ + + + + + + + + +

EQUAL RIGHTS FOR EVERYONE? REALLY!

(What follows was a poem written by the author.)

It was never the intent that a BENCH was meant for the homeless to sleep on. Its' intent was that JUSTICE would be served by whomever that bench is sat upon!

Unfortunately, what has been happenin' is that decisions are often being doled out … in an unfair and questionable manner. This, according to what I've both witnessed and also told about!

Therefore, I would be remiss not to repeat a quote that was recently said … by former U.S. Supreme Court Justice – Sandra Day O'Connor … that "JUSTICE IS MOSTLY DEAD!"

It has become BIG MONEY that too often decides most decisions from the bench! And it's also BIG MONEY that controls far too many others who are elected and told what to do by the one percent!

It's GREED that's INFECTING our DEMOCRACY and also AFFECTING most everyone!

Therefore, it's time that we remind ourselves of what Thomas Jefferson once said: "Equal rights are meant for all … special privileges for none!

MY BELIEF IN REINCARNATION

My belief in reincarnation has a lot to do with the reason I am waiting for an inmate to get out of prison; therefore my belief is not for any of the usual reasons and so read on!

I met him while working as a volunteer inside Auburn Prison in the 1970s and although many people won't be able to accept nor comprehend why I would ever get involved with a prisoner, let me explain anyway.

I first became aware of James Moore because I bought one of his 'Clipper Ship' paintings. *(I still possess the painting.)* I bought the painting of the clipper ship because I'd seen that same ship many times before in a re-occurring dream I'd had during my teen-age years! *(I later was told by a teacher of 'past-life regression' that "re-occurring dreams are very often indicators of a past life.")*

It was a year after I'd started working with the Auburn Jaycee Organization inside the prison that James Moore joined the group. After he joined, there were many occasions we sat together in both business meetings and committee meetings. Over the course of the three years of my involvement with the Jaycees, the interaction between both he and I would be considered strictly 'business-related'.

THE LONG PROCESS OF ACCEPTANCE

For years I'd been involved in the study of the paranormal but believing in *"reincarnation"* was among the hardest thing for me to accept. Despite reading extensively on the subject, it wasn't until the late 1970s, after attending workshops/seminars where credible people spoke on the *subject* that I began to believe that *maybe* it was possible.

As already indicated, it was in 1971 that this author organized a local parapsychology group that brought several like-minded credible professionals together to discuss and research a number of topics, including *"reincarnation"*. Our meetings were always open to the public.

Imagine the group's surprise when a Catholic priest came to the 'open' meeting ... he'd seen our publicized newspaper announcement that the topic was to be on *"reincarnation"*.

When the priest introduced himself, he said he wanted "to share with us what had happened at the 'Council of Nicea' in the year 325 A.D." He explained that "Emperor Constantine asked that the belief in reincarnation be taken away but several priests refused to sign the Creed and were subsequently banned from the Church." He informed the group that "until the fourth century, the belief in 'reincarnation' had existed in the Catholic Church." *(This was the first time most of us were aware of that important piece of history!)* The priest also told us that "despite the change in church law, many clergy privately believe in reincarnation" and then added that he to "believed in it."

Another guest who spoke before our group on the same subject was Dr. Frederick Foos, a Cornell University Professor of Languages, He was affiliated with the "Eckankar" movement that he'd joined during one of his frequent trips to California. *(He was responsible for introducing it into the Finger Lakes region.)* "Eckists believe in reincarnation," he told us.

Another guest, Dr. Creston Munger, Chairman of the English Department at the local Cayuga Community College, spoke to the group about the belief of "reincarnation" held by Buddhists.

The several *topics* the group covered over those three years were subsequently shared at the local YMCA over the two years that followed. All the proceeds generated from our workshops were donated to the "Y". *(The third year we brought the same ten-week series into Auburn Prison.)*

It was because of this author's continued disbelief in *reincarnation* that I realized it would probably take a few past-life experiences in order to be convinced of it and at that time I had yet to experience even one. But let me explain how I finally got to have the first one!

It began when James Moore sent me a Christmas card in 1979 that had a "symbol" on it which had special significance for me. *(Symbols are 'signs' which – for me – often have special meaning. I first became aware of their importance because Christ said to "be aware of signs.")*

Over time I also realized *'signs'* were sometimes answers to questions I was asking or warnings of things to come, etcetera. *(And after even more time, I've also come to realize that they could also be indicators associated with a past life'.)*

In his card Jim included a letter, 'thanking' me for all the work I'd "done on behalf of the inmates in the prison." He added his personal regrets about the adverse publicity being given in the local media about my personal involvement with Jerome Washington and that inmate's federal "Right to Write" case. *(The attorneys for the plaintiff said that the "testimony in the case – I'd given – was instrumental in the favorable decision given Mr. Washington")*

I did respond to Jim's letter letting him know I "would visit him on the next trip back to Auburn" and I did. It was on that first visit that I asked him a few questions about his life before the crime and also about the crime. He was honest and forthright in giving me honest answers to each question I asked.

When I asked him what kind of work he'd done prior to committing his crime in 1963? He answered that he'd "been a landscaper for several years." He also told me he'd "been under psychiatric care for 'episodes of mania' for two years prior to the commission of the crime" and then he was released by the psychiatrist and told, "there was nothing more that psychiatry was able to do *(for him)* since the condition was 'genetic/inherited'." *(He "believed that it was possible" since his mother "had been committed to an insane asylum" when he was in his early teens.")* Two months after being released from his psychiatric care, he committed the crime of murder during 'an episode of mania'!

(It's somewhat 'eerie' that Gowanda Insane Asylum – where Jim's mother was committed and also given those shock treatments back in the late 30's – that years later the facility became Gowanda Correctional Facility and Jim was transferred there for two years, in the late 1990's.)

What happened a few months after meeting Jim is what was the beginning of the confirmation process!

It was while working in Glens Falls that one day, I walked
into their public library and glanced over to the table where
the most recent books acquired by the library were on
exhibit. I was surprised to see Dr. Rachel Carson's book,
"Silent Spring" among them. *(I was surprised because her
book had already come out in the late 1960's and in my own
mind I questioned why in 1980 it would be appearing on the
table with new releases!)*

For whatever reason, I decided to pick the book up because I
had always intended to read it. As I stood in the check-out
line waiting, I happened to open the book and on the page I
opened to … the word *"dieldrin"* stood out. As I read the
paragraph describing *"the chemical used by landscapers and
then subsequently banned because of its mind-altering side
effects', including episodes of mania"* … that I immediately
knew I'd found the underlying cause of Jim's unexplained
'episodes of mania'!

After I checked out the book, I made copies of the pages of
that chapter and left the library. I immediately drove to the
post office and asked for *a stamped, legal-sized envelope*
and inserted the copied pages. After sealing the envelope, I
addressed it to Jim at Auburn prison.

I knew the weight of the several pages would mean
additional postage and so asked the clerk to check the weight
and let me know what that would be? After weighing it she
said "it requires an additional 14 cent stamp." She passed
the stamp to me. Much to my surprise the stamp had Dr.
Carson's picture on it! *(Here was a 'confirming sign' that
this was Jim's answer and I realized also that 'spirit' was
helping.)*

I asked the clerk when they'd gotten the new stamps and she replied, "the stamps came in today."

When I saw Jim on my next trip back to Auburn, he thanked me for my letter because he now had an answer to the unexplained episodes he'd been having over the several years he'd been doing landscaping. *(The episodes had stopped soon after he came into prison. According to Dr. Carson, "they would stop but only if the chemical wasn't being handled any longer." As the reader may know, she was the recipient of the Nobel Prize in Chemistry!)*

MY TRIP TO THE UNITED KINGDOM

It was on a trip to England that summer that I experienced my first *past-life* recall. I was a guest of the Greenes. The couple was paying all my expenses. *(They were also Spiritualists and had attended one of my workshops at the Freeville Spiritualist Campgrounds where - at that time - I was on the board of trustees.)* Over time, we became friends!

The dates they picked for the trip were connected to their scheduled appointment – made the year before – with a famous *spiritual healer* in Wales … Mr. George Chapman.

Upon our arrival at Heathrow Airport, we rented a car and headed out of London toward our first night's *bed and breakfast* destination.

The next morning we left for Wales. En-route, I sensed that we were near a place that was only a short distance off the main route we were on and asked if we might make a detour? *(I sensed 'spirit' was influencing and told them so.)*

As we approached one of the bends in the road, I blurted out, "stop just around the next curve because I'm sensing there's a ruined castle ahead" and sure enough, it was there ... visible from the road.

Why I sensed its familiarity ... I didn't know, but I felt it! I hurried up to the top of the hill and ran across the courtyard to steps that took me below ... taking me down to what had been the dungeon. Suddenly I realized ... I remembered this place!

The feeling that came over me was indescribable. Immediately I experienced great pain and I saw faces around me and it included the face of a soldier. It was Jim's face! Unexplained welts began to erupt all over my body. I then realized that I had experienced all of what was happening before – but in another lifetime!

That particular lifetime was when I was a nun in the 1500's when Henry VIII broke away from the Catholic Church because he was told by the Pope that he "could not marry again" and so, in 1536 the King "enacted the first 'Act of Union' which permitted the political and legal union of England and Wales." Wales fell under the English shire system and the first destruction of the monasteries began. The killing of all priests and nuns occurred as well. Henry VIII became the head of the Episcopal Church.

When what I was experiencing began to subside and I was able to compose myself, I made it back up the stone stairway … but with great difficulty. The Greenes were waiting in the courtyard and upon seeing me were startled at my disheveled appearance and asked, "what happened?" And, I told them.

Back on the road again, we continued on to our scheduled *bed and breakfast* stop where we were able to get some ice to apply on various areas of my body that were swollen. It was fortunate that Alice had brought along some strong pain medication because it limited the discomfort I was experiencing and after it took effect, I was able to finally fall asleep.

THE APPOINTMENT WITH THE HEALER

The usual wait time to get an appointment with Mr. George Chapman was typically <u>one year</u>. He was a spiritual healer working in partnership with Dr. William Lang, an English surgeon who had died a few decades previous. It is Chapman's belief that "Dr. Lang is able to bring about healing" through his intercession. According to the testimony of many doctors, "some of their more difficult patients were healed by George Chapman" and their testimonies are included in Chapman's book: "<u>Surgeon From Another World</u>".

I accompanied the Greenes that next morning to Chapman's House in Pant Glas, Tre'r-ddol, Machynlleth, Mid Wales.

Alice was already in with George Chapman when the phone rang at the desk of the receptionist. Because of where I was sitting, I was able to understand that the caller was canceling his or her appointment. Upon hanging up the phone, the receptionist asked me if I "would like the appointment that has just been canceled" and I said, "yes!" I then asked if I "might know the name of the caller" and he replied, "a Mr. James Moore."

THAT WAS THE 'CONFIRMING SIGN' I NEEDED TO TELL ME THAT IT WAS JIM I'D SEEN THE DAY BEFORE ... "THE SOLDIER WHO HAD KILLED ME!"

Upon entering the darkened room where the 'healings' take place, I sensed a peace I'd never experienced before. I was told "to be seated and to close my eyes and be still."

Even with my eyes closed, behind my eye lids I was aware of a cascading of light which wrapped itself around my entire body. I sensed a 'pulling out of the body' the still existing pain in those swollen areas of my body. It was an experience that seemed to last only seconds ... yet I was told later by the Greenes that I'd "been with George Chapman a very long time." (Apparent to all was the disappearance of all the swellings!)

Hardly a word was spoken among the three of us as we made the trip back toward London that day. We stopped for supper before continuing the short distance to our next night's stay at a bed and breakfast.

We arrived at the Bretforton Hall Clinic at Vale of Evesham, Worcestershire shortly before our scheduled appointments with Dr. Peter Guy Manners. We were escorted into the garden area where his assistant had asked us to wait.

(I had met Dr Manner back in Auburn a few years earlier when he spoke at the local college on the topic: "Cymatics: Using Sound for Healing". He was already recognized around the world for his extensive research in the field. He was both a physicist and a medical doctor. After he spoke, he met privately with members of our parapsychology group, telling us about some of the paranormal experiences he'd had. He showed us impressive photos of Kirlian photography he'd taken. They were the first the group had ever seen, showing proof of the aura around human bodies.

When Dr. Manners appeared in the garden area and introduced himself to the Greenes, he shook all of our hands and then he turned to me and said, "so, what did you pick up about the garden?" I responded, *"I sensed the presence of monks who had once walked on these grounds."* He said I was *"correct"* and then asked that I *"come with him and then the Greenes will come next."*

I followed him into his office and upon sitting, he began to speak. He assured me that he *"had talked to no one"* and *"that as a clairvoyant"* he was *"aware that on the previous day of (my) having had an experience of recalling something from a past life."* (*Needless to say I was surprised both by what he was saying and also, that he was admitting to being 'a clairvoyant'!)*

As he opened the top drawer of his desk he said, *"I am going to show you an anatomy chart and on it I have already placed X's which correspond to places on your body where you sustained injuries in a previous lifetime."* He handed me the paper and to my utter amazement he'd already marked areas on the chart where swellings occurred during the recent episode where I'd had that 'past life' experience.

Dr. Manner went on to say that only a few knew about his *psychic ability.* He then said, *"It's because it takes one to know one that I knew back when I was in Auburn that you were also a clairvoyant. That is why I invited you to come here if you ever came to England."* But then he added, *"I was sure you would come one day."*

He went on to tell me that he wanted me to become a cymatics technician because it would help in my development as a *'healer'*. However, at that time I wasn't convinced that was something I could do but he assured me it would come as I added the 'tools' that I needed in order to enhance my ability to be a 'healer' … "becoming a channel which allows healing to come through."

I told him about recognizing the face of the officer who'd killed me in a previous lifetime because it was someone I presently knew in Auburn prison. I then told him about the coincidence that someone named "James Moore" had canceled their appointment so that I got to have a *healing* done by George Chapman. He explained to me that *"it was no coincidence that the names happened to be the same … sometimes we have confirmations of our past lives given to us in these strange and mysterious ways."*

He assured me that *"there is an important reason why the two of you are together in this lifetime and part of the reason is that you need to also forgive him for what he did to you in that lifetime."* He then told me, *"you needed that healing because it was to let you to know that healing is possible … but only possible through a higher power that brings it through the 'healer's hands' … it's how we can become the channels for healing."*

(Jim later told me that I appeared to him in his cell during the time I was in England. Thus I had another 'out-of-body' experience which (to-date) I never recall having the knowledge of having done it! However, Dr. Manner later wrote me that it would have probably happened in view of what I was experiencing in England at that same time.)

And so, after the completion of my training with Dr. Manner, both in England and later in Boston, when he came again to the U.S. to teach and to lecture, and ultimately I became a *Cymatic Technician* and am registered with the *National Association of Healers*. Although I did not actively involve myself in this newly acquired training, it did play an important role later in this life. It had particular relevancy because I trained two chiropractors and one medical doctor, who enhanced their practices with it.

AN EXPLANATION OF "CYMATICS"

History tells us that the use of sound waves for curative purposes was practiced in ancient times. Their modern day use by medical science is able to offer greater benefit. Different sound frequencies – *harmonic computations* – having been found, affect different parts of the body and its chemistry. After the diagnosis, treatment is directed to the areas of diseased tissues and bones and other areas of the body either by an applicator that transmits the sound directly to the treated area and/or by hearing the correct frequencies by simply listening to them. Sound waves of frequencies higher than those in the audible range are still being experimented with as curative agents.

Dr. Manner points out that *"the range of sound waves above the audible level can be very destructive in their nature and, unfortunately, are – at the present time – being experimented with for military and similar purposes ... i.e. torture."*

What is important for the reader to understand is that each molecule of which an organ or a tissue is composed, has its own individual sound pattern and emits a vibration peculiar to this pattern. A healthy organ will have its molecules working together in a harmonious relationship with each other, and all will be of the same pattern. If different sound patterns enter the organ, the harmonious relationship could be upset. If these frequencies are weak in their vibrations, they will be overcome by the stronger vibrations of the native ones. If the foreign ones prove to be the stronger on the other hand, they may establish their discordant pattern in the organ, bone, tissue, etc. and this is what we call *'disease'*. Therefore, a *'cymatics'* treatment contains a harmonic frequency pattern which will reinforce the frequency of the organ. The vibrations of the intruders will be neutralized and the correct pattern for that organ re-established.

BACK TO THE PROOF OF "REINCARNATION"

The belief in reincarnation had to have been what Jesus believed because He said, we *"reap what we sow"* and since payback might not happen in just one lifetime, it would surely come in a subsequent one!

(As a child I had difficulty understanding why someone might be born handicapped. After all, isn't GOD 'a loving GOD' and if so, why would HE allow a baby to born handicapped? Even Helen Keller accepted her blindness and deafness as a circumstance of 'cause and effect' from a previous lifetime and it is her belief that helped me understand why reincarnation was possible.)

Because the belief of *reincarnation* also exists in Buddhism, it was possible for me to study the subject matter in more depth. At the Buddhist Educational and Retreat Center in Soquel, California where I worked as a volunteer over a three year period in the 1990's, I was able to find a wealth of information on the subject.

I am also convinced that ones' own genealogy can provide clues to lifetimes we might have had on our own family tree. The years of investigative work on my own family's genealogy has provided a few clues as to who I was before.

Returning to a place where an ancestor had once lived will often bring back some recall, if you'd been the one there in a past life. This happened for me twice. It happened in the Plymouth Colony when I entered the hut my ancestors had lived in and then again, when I entered the abandoned school house where my great grandmother had once attended and later taught. (*This explains why – as a young child – I'd had 'recurring dreams' about being a school teacher in a one-room school house. Perhaps that was me?*)

Having the knowledge of *hypnotherapy* has allowed me to occasionally access a past life by doing *'self-regression'.* It has also given me an opportunity to find my own answers rather than having someone else tell me who I might have been in my previous lifetimes. Accessing your own memories is the best way to find the truth. Sometimes it's also important to understand why certain life experiences come to us in this life, as well as connecting it to a past life.

(I am a BIG believer in self-hypnosis and not just for the above stated reason but because one can learn how to control pain and bleeding with that knowledge. Meditation puts one into a relaxed state that is known as a state of 'alpha' and it is the 'alpha' state when someone is in hypnosis. Being relaxed not only reduces tension but 'answers' often come when meditating. Even Christ said, to … "be still and know".)

It has been the numerous *past-life recalls* I've had that <u>finally</u> convinced me of *reincarnation.* One has to be a 'truth seeker' in order to get answers and that's not always an easy thing to do. For me it has meant unlocking my mind by reaching beyond its once limited boundaries. And so, call it destiny that brought me from the outside to the inside of Auburn prison.

It's because of coming inside that both Jim and I can now tell our story. But it's even more than that! It definitely is a past life connection with James Moore that is the reason I'm waiting. It's already been over forty (40) years I've waited and it's also the reason this writer felt it necessary to include "<u>Why I Wait</u>" as a chapter in this book.

HAVE YOU LIVED BEFORE ?

Although 'past life regression' can be done by a trained hypnotherapist, what follows is a self-test for those who may want to get some insight into their former lives.

- If you have ever walked into a strange building and have instinctively known your way around, displayed a talent for music, writing or art, that other family members don't have, or suffered from a fear that has no rational basis? Then you are drawing on experiences from a previous life.
- Do you have recurring dreams you can't explain? The fact that dream researchers report that people who have recurring dreams may be reliving a traumatic experience from a previous life.
- If you feel instantly drawn to someone on first meeting? You probably knew that person before.

- Some people often feel drawn to a certain country and if they travel there, they feel as if they are returning home. *(Or if you long for a certain country or a type of setting, such as a home near the ocean or in the mountains, it could mean you probably had a happy life there before.)*
- Do you hate alcohol or something else so strongly that you cannot tolerate even its smell? If you have such a strong aversion to drink, you may have been an alcoholic in a former life.
- Do you sometimes experience depression or strange foreboding at a certain time of the year and cannot understand why? Or, if a certain season of the year triggers such thoughts, it could be the time of the year when you once suffered a traumatic experience or a very untimely death.
- Sometimes you might take up causes or experience feelings far different from what would be expected of you, given the way you were brought up. Or, you might be puzzled by the path you have chosen in life and the purpose of your lifestyle. *(In my own case I discovered through hypnosis that the reason I had devoted most of my life to righting social injustice was I had been a slave in a former life.)*
- You have conscious memories of living before. *(Some people can actually recall events, even without hypnosis or meditation, of other lives.)*
- Do you ever find yourself doing and saying things which seem completely out of character for the person you think you are? *(The experts say personality traits from a former life can resurface.*

A technique that can sometimes work is to 'record all dreams' on a pad you keep by the side of the bed. Pay attention to the clothing you're wearing in the dream and a time period, if you recall it. Sometimes, when eating an apple … you'll recall a 'past life' event.

You should list your *likes and dislikes* because they sometimes give you clues to your past life.

For example: As a child the only food I had any dislike of was 'rice'! Of interest was that during my training to become a hypnotherapist, it was in a past-life-recall session with the instructor that I was able to recall being poor and living in China.

+ + + + + + + + +

What is also a bit of irony is the fact that my grandmother's maiden name was: Rice ... and as a child I felt a strong attachment to her. She'd even saved my life when I was an infant ... something I was never aware of until my oldest sister told me prior to her demise in 2001... that I was 'close to death' due to having whooping cough when I was an infant. And, because my mother did not believe in doctors – said "if GOD wants to take her, let her go!" But my grandmother pleaded with her and said that she'd take me home with her ... and she did! Over the course of at least a year I stayed with my grandmother. I was held a lot and was given goat's milk. And it's obvious that I made it!)

+ + + + + + + + + + + + + + + +

ORDAINED A 'SPIRITUALIST' MINISTER AND THE BAPTISM PROMISE

FROM THE OUTSIDE – GOING IN

It was at the direction of my spiritual teacher, Reverend Mae Merritt York that I *"could best fulfill my requirements for my ordination by working with prison inmates."* She felt that I *"needed to break down barriers that existed between me and 'my brothers' and have a first-hand experience of why the need to understand 'forgiveness'."* She believed that because I had grown up in Auburn, New York where the first electric chair was used in the United States that *"it was obvious that the difficulties I was having to forgive those in my own life might be lessened if I went among those who were guilty of the same issues I was dealing with."*

It is important to mention that one of the *twenty-eight points* that State Commissioner Russell G. Oswald agreed to after the Attica *riot* was that "service organizations, churches, agencies, etc. help institute realistic, effective rehabilitation programs for all inmates according to their offense and personal needs."

I soon discovered — *as did all volunteers* — that inmates were hungry to be listened to seriously, to be believed, to be respected, to be cared about, to be liked and to be dealt with honestly. It is an exciting and exhilarating experience to talk to a prison audience. They are a keen, critical, and merciless group. Their beliefs, ideals and preferences had to be examined and understood *(perhaps not agreed with but nevertheless understood).*

I realized too, it was important to neither approve nor disapprove of why these men were there but that I should first try to comprehend some of the issues and consequences of their behavior.

CONTINUING THE JOURNEY TOWARD ORDINATION

As I continued the journey to become an ordained Spiritualist minister, I became aware that the path to spiritual epiphany offers a potpourri of offerings which includes Pentecostal healing services, Kabbalah dabbling, crystal gazing, Sufi prayer techniques, Eucharistic adoration, card readings, yoga, tantric sex – and so many more that are on the table. And for most, it becomes a pleasant hobby than a transformative vocation. <u>I've looked at most of them</u>!

Certainly religious freedom is guaranteed to all Americans and the *thousands* of Protestant *sects* that exist in this country today is so unfortunate because it is their often slight differences that are causing turmoil among themselves! The fact that today's translations can be interpreted in so many ways is because of the hundreds of translations of the Bible that have occurred since it was translated from Aramaic into Greek and then into Latin. In 1534 Martin Luther upset the Pope by translating it into German. *(It was only the priests that knew Greek and Latin and due to the lack of education of the people, they only believed the dictates of the Church.)*

The "Religious Reformation" began when Luther translated the Bible into German and the translation into English followed shortly thereafter. *(Numerous translations into English occurred prior to the <u>King James</u> version of the Bible in the 17th Century.)* The <u>King James</u> version was considered the biggest improvement over the many others that had been previously written. In recent years there's been a number of re-writes of the <u>King James</u> version. More recently the <u>New Living Bible</u> came out and is used by many.

Certainly when the *New Living Bible* came out in July 1971, it too was a much easier read.

Personally, my preference is the *Holy Bible* from the Ancient Eastern Text written by George M. Lamsa, who in 1933 translated it from the language Jesus spoke – *the Aramaic (Syric) text* – which was also Dr. Lamsa's native tongue. *(The Aramaic Scriptures are also called "The Peshitta.")* There are subtle differences in it and in a few instances, some major differences!

Dr. Lamsa was a native Assyrian and was reared in that part of the ancient biblical land from which Abraham migrated to Palestine. He studied under the teachers of his tribe and then later, he advanced his studies by attending the Archbishop of Canterbury's College in Persia and Turkey. After the First World War, he continued his studies in the Virginia Theological Seminary in Alexandria, Virginia.

Dr. Lamsa said that he *"corrected crucial mistranslations due to the confusion of letters and words by translators who had approached the complexities of Aramaic grammar without the abilities of a native speaker."*

The example given on the book's jacket is taken from Matthew 6:13 which in the *King James Version* it reads: *"And lead us not into temptation, but deliver us from evil."* It is rendered in the Lamsa translation as: *"And do not let us enter into temptation, but deliver us from evil."*

Another example given is taken from Matthew 19:14, which reads: *"And again I say unto you, it is easier for a camel to go through the eye of the needle, than for a rich man to enter into the kingdom of God."* Lamsa corrects it to: *"Again I say to you, it is easier for a rope to go through the eye of a needle, than for a rich man to enter into the kingdom of God."*

These two examples are indicated for the benefit of the reader who may want to consider reviewing the reading of the *Bible* as Dr. Lamsa has translated it.

What is unfortunate is that the numerous translations of the *Bible* has allowed too many the right to how they want to interpret it. Unfortunately a conflict arises when their interpretations aren't in accord with how others interpret it! *(No wonder we have thousands of Protestant sects in this country today!)*

What Jonathan Swift said in *"Thoughts on Various Subjects"* (1706) is even truer today because *"we have just enough religion to make us hate, but not enough to make us love one another."*

As a member of the clergy, I studied world religions. All of them preach *love and service* underneath their superficial particulars. I've also come to realize that religion is a personal relationship with … what I prefer to say … *"Infinite Wisdom."* What we need to remember is that religion should be taken *metaphorically* and not *literally.*

We need to also remember that *"doing unto others as you would have them do unto you"* is what *Christ* preached. Unfortunately, mankind has made it so unnecessarily confusing!

HOW RELIGION IS LOOKED AT BY OTHERS

It couldn't be more simply put than how Abraham Lincoln interpreted his own religious belief when cornered by the news media who questioned why he "did not go to church?" He told them, "When I do good, I feel good and when I do bad, I feel bad ... and that gentlemen is my religion." *(He then walked away.)*

Even the Dalai Lama ... when asked by the media in 2015 about his own religion, said: *"kindness is my religion."*

It's because <u>Freedom of Religion</u> is guaranteed under our *"Bill of Rights"* that we should be allowed to practice our faiths open-mindedly but to be tolerant of different beliefs also.

Unfortunately, there's too much bias/prejudice with too many folks and it just isn't possible – *for most* – to practice as they should be able to. *(Look at what is happening with Muslims in the U.S., as well as in other parts of the world today!)* Nevertheless, it's best to remind ourselves that to be *free* of our own bias/prejudices is a 'blessing' and if other folks want to possess bias and prejudices, then it belongs to them! *(The Scripture reminds us "there are none so blind as those who do not see the truth!")*

INTERPRETATIONS DIFFER

Although I can personally cite many *examples* of what I *personally* believe is an incorrect belief held in the minds of many Protestant sects, it is the one that follows that best illustrates one such *example*:

My son married a woman who, as a child, attended a church she still attends. One of the 'dictates' of that church is that *"girls should not go to college".*

And so, when their seventeen year old daughter came home with a letter from a reputable state college in New York that indicated that she was being *"awarded a full scholarship that also included room and board"*... her parents' reaction was to tell her*"to pack her suitcase and immediately move out!"* *(And she did move out that day! She slept on her girlfriend's porch for the remainder of the summer! And, although the parents turned their back on her for a very long time ... they eventually came around when she was graduating with a Master's degree from Buffalo University!)*

Certainly their religious beliefs might meet with many who question that church's *dogmas and creeds* … it is mentioned here as an *'example'* of how different churches can be!

THE MANY TRANSLATIONS OF THE BIBLE

Let me point out also that today's religious scholars are aware that *the original Bible was first written in Aramaic and then Hebrew and Greek*. And, since its first release, it is the *Bible* that holds the record for being the most translated literary work in history!

According to the website, Bible Study News: "No one can give you an exact number for the English translations and paraphrases of the Bible printed since Tyndale's New Testament of 1522. The number of printed English translations and paraphrases of the Bible, whether complete or not, is about 900." (Nine hundred is what it is!)

Not until a few decades ago did Dr. George Lamsa – with the knowledge of Aramaic translate the only one of the original texts written in Aramaic into English. His translation is now in wide use today and is considered the more reliable version. Lamsa was born and raised where *Christ* was raised and where the Aramaic language is still spoken today, also as it was spoken at the time *Christ* was on this earth.

In Lamsa's translation he explains his interpretation of the scripture of his *Bible* figuratively and not literal.

Here are just a few examples:

Bible: Gen.1:3 "Let there be light" vs. Lamsa's
  interpretation – "Let there be enlightenment."

Bible: Ex.3:2 "The burning bush was not consumed. vs.
  Lamsa's interpretation – "There are difficulties ahead
  but difficulties will be overcome."

Bible: John 1:18 "He is the only begotten son." vs.
  Lamsa's interpretation: "He was the first one who
  recognized the fatherhood of God. The only God-like
  man; hence, a spiritual son of God."

Bible: John 3:3 "Be born again." vs. Lamsa's interpretation:
  "Become like a child, to start all over."

Bible: John 10:36 "I and my Father are one" vs.
  Lamsa's interpretation: "The Father and I agree."

In several verses of both his version, as well as today's translations, it mentions "judging others." It's referenced in: Isaiah 66:5, Ezekiel 16:52-56, Luke 6:37, Romans 2:1,2, Romans 14:3,4,10-13, Corinthians 4:3-5, James 3:1 and James 4:11,12.

Therefore, it is important that we not always believe what others dictate as their interpretation(s) of the *Bible* as being the sole 'gospel truth' … perhaps it is best to do some 'checking-out' for ourselves and find what is a more correct interpretation. For this writer, Lamsa comes the closest!

THE BURNT OVER DISTRICT

According to Wikipedia: *"The burned-over district was the religious scene in the western and central regions of New York in the early 19th century, where religious revivals and Pentecostal movements of the Second Great Awakening took place."* The term *"burnt district"* was coined by Charles Grandison Finner who in his 1876 book - *Autobiography of Charles G. Finney* – referred to a *burnt district,* denoting an area in central and Western New York State during the Second Great Awakening. The name was inspired by the notion that the area had been so heavily evangelized as to have no "fuel" *(unconverted population)* left over to "burn" *(convert).*

In this instance, "religion is related to reform movements of the period, such as abolition, women's rights and utopian social experiements" and the region expanded to include areas of Central New York that were important to them.

Western New York spawned a number of innovative religious movements, all founded by laypeople during the early 19th century. They included:

The *Latter Day Saint* movement aka: The Church of Jesus Christ of Latter-day Saints. *(Joseph Smith lived in the region and prior to discovering the 'golden plates' near Palmyra, New York, he did carpentry work in the Auburn area ... including the home of Mr. William Seward, Secretary of State under President Lincoln's administration..)*

One of the more noteable papers of the time can be found in Volume V of the Rochester Historical Society's 'Publication Fund Series'. The text of Adelbert Croninse's paper entitled: *"The Beginnings of Modern Spiritualism In and Near Rochester"* was read before the society on October 29, 1925.

104 POSSIBILITIES

He stated that: *"although not a paper on 'Spiritualism' that came from many sources, the fact that the two great movements, Mormonism and Modern Spiritualism, had their origins in the same locality and at so nearly the same time."*

There was also the movement called: *Adventism (aka: Seven Day Adventists),* founded by William Miller, a farmer who lived in Low Hampton, New York, who preached that the literal *Second Coming* would occur "October 22, 1844."

The *Shakers* were also active in the area, with their first communal farm established in Central New York.

There was also the *Oneida Society*. It was a large utopian group that established a successful community in Central New York that subsequently disbanded. It was known for its unique interpretation of group marriage which had mates chosen by committee and offspring of the community raised in common.

Although the Fox sisters of Hydesville, New York were given credit for leading the American movement of *Spiritualism* in 1848, it was the "Auburn Circle" that held the first "circles" *(aka: seances)* that same year with the Fox sisters in attendance. The American movement of *Spiritualism* was centered in the retreat at Lily Dale and a few years later in Freeville where *"communion with the dead was demonstrated and taught."*

It is the Freeville Campgrounds where the author served several terms on the board of directors. During summers the author and several others conducted workshops in the field of parapsychology, all were well attended by the public.

The author also did private 'readings' at the Campgrounds.

It is also important to mention that in addition to the extensive religious activity, the burned-over district was also

famous for social radicalism. Elizabeth Cady Stanton, the
early feminist, a resident of Seneca Falls and where she and
others in the community initiated the Seneca Falls
Convention devoted to women's suffrage.

THE UNIVERSAL CHURCH OF THE MASTER – UCM

My religious affiliation – since 1974 – is with *The Universal
Church of the Master* that has its offices in San Jose,
California, located at 1361 So. Winchester Boulevard. Their
website is: www.u-c-m.org and the reader is encouraged to
check the website out to learn more about the organization
that has members and churches around the world.

Over the course of a decade, I completed the requirements
for ordination and flew to California where I was ordained in
1984 by the then President, Reverend Birdie Petersen *(now
deceased)*.

Worth mentioning is what I realized when receiving my
ordination papers in my post office mailbox after returning
back to New York State from my trip to California.

The post office in Auburn, New York is a building that was
built on the site of where the First Baptist Church once
stood. It was also the church I attended throughout my
childhood. I was also baptized in the church font when I
was twelve years old.

It was upon opening the letter from UCM – containing my
Certificate of Ordination that I realized – *for the very first
time* – that I was actually standing over the exact spot where
the church font once stood. I also recalled at that same
moment that it was during that baptism that I made a
promise to myself that I *"would one day become a member
of the clergy"*... and it became so! *(This is again one of
many 'confirmations' of what the author has experienced*

106   POSSIBILITIES

many times throughout in my life and further proof of what is possible and also, that what you wish for can come true!)

From 1989 to 1998, I lived in Santa Cruz, California and while living there I also completed the requirements for a doctorate degree in Naturopathy. I did so while donating hundreds of hours to UCM. When I worked in the office, I also served on the UCM board of directors as Treasurer. I was also the editor of UCM's quarterly magazine.

As I look back at the several years that I was involved as a member of the clergy, it is the time spent among the prisoners that I believe my efforts were most appreciated. The greatest need for *"doing unto others"* -- as Jesus the Christ, Sidhartha the Buddha and Mohammed taught – is doing it inside a prison!

+ + + + + + + + +

Worth mentioning also is that after spending three years volunteering my time at a Buddhist Retreat and Educational Center in Soquel, California in the 90's, I was able to greatly enhance my Christian beliefs by being exposed to the Mahayana teachings of Buddhism because Jesus' words closely parallels the Dhammapada, the central book to Buddhists.

Here are only a few examples of the hundreds that can be found in the Dhammapada:

*(1)   Luke 2:31   Do unto others as you would have them do to you.
          Dhammapada 10:1   Consider others as yourself.*

(2)   Luke: 6:29   If anyone strikes you on the cheek, offer the other also.

Majjhima Nikaya 21:6   If anyone should give you a blow with his hand, with a stick, or with a knife, you should abandon any desires and utter no evil words.

(3)   Luke 6:27-30   Love your enemies, do good to those who hate you, bless those who curse you, pray for those who abuse you. From anyone who takes away your coat, do not withhold even your shirt. Give to everyone who begs from you; and if anyone takes away your goods, do not ask for them again.

Dhammapada 1:5 and 17:3   Hatreds do not ever cease in this world by hating, but by love; this is an eternal truth. Overcome anger by love, overcome evil by good. Overcome the miser by giving, overcome the liar by truth.

(4)   Matthew 26:52   Put your sword back into its place; for all those who take the sword will perish by the sword.

Digha Nikaya 1:1.8   Abandoning the taking of life, the ascetic Guatama (Believer) dwells refraining from taking life, without stick or sword.

(5)   Mark 10:19   You shall not murder; you shall not commit adultery; you shall not steal; you shall not bear false witness; you shall not defraud.

Khuddakapatha 2   Abstain from killing and from taking what is not given. Abstain from unchastity and from speaking falsely. Do not accept gold and silver.

(6)   Luke 6:41-42   Why do you see the speck in your neighbor's eye, but do not notice the log in your own eye? Or how can you say to your neighbor, "Friend, let me take the speck out of your eye," when you yourself do not see the log in your own eye? You hypocrite, first take the log out of

your own eye, and then you will see clearly to take the speck out of your neighbor's eye.

Udanavarga 27:1   The faults of others are easier to see than one's own; the faults of others are easily seen, for they are sifted like chaff, but one's own faults are hard to see. This is like the cheat who hides his dice and shows the dice of his opponent, calling attention to the other person's shortcomings, continually thinking of accusing him.

Dhammapada 4:7 Do not look at the faults of others, or what others have done or not done; observe what you yourself have done and have not done.

(7)   Luke 4:13 When the devil had finished every test, he departed from him until an opportune time.

Lalitavistara Sutra 18   During the six years the Bodhisattva (Guatama) practiced austerities, the demon followed him step-by-step, seeking an opportunity to harm him. But he found no opportunity whatsoever and went away discouraged and discontent.

(8)   John 11:26 Everyone who lives and believes in me will never die.

Majjhima Nikaya 22:45 Those who have sufficient faith in me, sufficient love for me, are all headed for heaven or beyond.

(9)   Matthew 8:16 That evening they brought to him many who were possessed with demons; and he cast out the evil spirits with a word, and cured all who were sick.

Samyutta Nikaya 46:14   The venerable Kassapa was sick and afflicted, stricken with a sore disease. Guatama the Buddha spoke to him and Kassaa was delighted. Then and there he rose from his sickness and abandoned all pain.

(10)   Luke 7:21-22   Jesus cured many people of diseases, plagues, and evil spirits, and gave sight to many who were blind. And he said to them, "Go and tell John what you have witnessed: the blind received their sight, the lame walk, the lepers are cleansed, the deaf hear, the dead are raised, the poor have good news brought to them."

Lalitavistra Sutra 7   As soon as the Bodhisattva was born, the sick were cured; the hungry and thirsty were no longer oppressed by hunger and thirst. Those maddened by drink lost their obsession. The mad recovered their senses, the blind regained their sight, and the deaf once more could hear. The halt and the lame obtained perfect limbs, the poor gained riches, and the prisoners were delivered of their bonds.

(11)   Mark 6:7 and 12:13   He called the twelve disciples and began to send them out two by two, and gave them the authority over the unclean/evil spirits. So they went out and proclaimed that all should repent. They cast out many demons, and anointed with oil many who were sick and cured them.

Vinaya, Mahavagga I:11.1 Walk, monks, throughout the land for the blessing of the people, for the happiness of the people, and out of compassion for the world, bless and anoint with oil those who are sick and cure them also.

WHAT SHOULD BE OBVIOUS TO THE READER IS THAT THE VERSES PARALLEL CLOSELY ... ONE WITH THE OTHER ... THEREFORE, IT'S REALLY A MATTER OF 'SAMANTICS' ... THEY ARE SAYING THE SAME THING!

+ + + + + + + + + + + + + +

WHAT I PERSONALLY BELIEVE!

THE BIRTH OF CHRIST

I would be remiss if I didn't tell my version of the 'birth of Christ' as I believe it to be!

History tells us that the three wise men came from India. *(The song, "We Three Kings" tells us that also. The opening verse in the Chapter of Matthew – Living Bible Edition – states that they were also 'astrologers'.)*

At that time in history, astrology was believed by the Jews and in India, the Buddhist philosophy was also practiced by all. *(Buddhists that were knowledgeable in astrology and considered 'enlightened' were known as 'rinpoches' and also considered 'clairvoyants'.)*

It would have been King Herod's men who were positioned at lookout posts on the hills outside of Bethlehem that would have seen the caravan approaching. They would have reported back to him that it was "not an ordinary caravan" that was approaching but instead, "a caravan that was coming by several camels... displaying great wealth ... and certainly a caravan that was coming from the orient!"

Those who have studied Buddhism know that they were 'rinpoches' who were making the trip because 'the star was a sign of the birth' ... of an *enlightened child*!

Buddhists also are aware that because the rinpoches *(aka: wise men)* were clairvoyants, they would be able to locate the child without asking!

When they found Mary and Joseph and the baby, they gave them the gifts of gold, myrrh and frankincense. *(The gold would enable the couple to make the trip out of the country –*

to Egypt – where they were to wait for the return of the three 'wise men'. The incense offered was for two reasons: one was to ward off evil spirits and the other, inviting only the good ones.) They did not stay long because they didn't want King Herod to know they'd already found the child!

When the three 'rinpoches' arrived at Herod's palace, they were immediately invited in. Herod would have already been aware that his guests believed in *astrology* and aware of the significance of the star; thus the obvious reason they were there! *(Herod was also aware that the Jews believed the star was the foretelling of the birth of a king.)* And so, when the rinpoches asked Herod, "if he'd found the child?" ... he responded, "no." The wise men would have certainly asked for at least a few nights rest *since they'd traveled so far* and would have – *no doubt* – stayed long enough to allow for Mary and Joseph to make the trip safely to Egypt!

Upon the departure of the wise men, King Herod put out the 'edif' *(order)* to have *"all baby boys ... age 3 and under ... killed!"* *(Evidence exists among Jewish writings that indicate that this event actually occurred!)*

There are Buddhists who know the village where Jesus was raised by Mary and Joseph in India but are reluctant to tell its' location because they believe it is their *'secret'* to keep. Those who have studied Buddhism see many parallels in Jesus teachings and their own belief system.

HIS CRUCIFIXION – AS I UNDERSTAND IT

During the brief time that Jesus was on this earth, besides healing the sick, he devoted himself to teaching **'forgiveness'** ... and as a result, **he had to prove he could do it!**

It was no accident that he set himself up to be captured! He knew what he must do and so he called upon his disciple, Judas to notify the authorities of where he could be found!

(Judas was no traitor!! He was simply doing what Jesus asked him to do! The act of throwing away the silver coins that were given to him for 'turning Christ in' is further proof!)

By being crucified ... Jesus proved he could do what he said *'we all must do'* ... to forgive! He had no other choice but to let himself be crucified ... if he was to be the 'example' he professed to be.

(So-o-o often when I've counseled some who might say they  *"wished they could be more perfect" ... I've usually responded: "if you were 'perfect' ... then you could be*  *guaranteed a crucifixtion!")*

The real irony is we call our country *"a Christian nation"* and yet we're one of the remaining three countries who still have the death penalty ... the others are: China and Iran!

+ + + + + + + + + + + +

Is it any wonder we're looked upon by

other nations and religions as being 'hypocrites'!

+ + + + + + + + + + +

PERSONAL STORIES – PARANORMAL ONES!

A TRUE MOUSE STORY

This is one of several personal accounts of events which are paranormal in nature and this one is probably one of the most unbelievable stories involving a mouse! *(Fortunately I don't panic when I see them.)*

It occurred inside Auburn Prison. It happened on the same day that one of the inmates in my class was chiding me about being a Christian. *(I always wore my crucifix around my neck whenever I went in.)* I knew he was a Muslim ...most of the men in the class were. *(I also knew the reason the man chiding me was in prison.)* Finally I responded to his chiding. I asked him to outstretch his arms and show me both of his hands ... which he did. I told him I thought he should feel fortunate that he possessed both hands because if he were in a country where his belief system ruled, his hands would have been both cut off since his crimes involved stealing on at least two occasions. *(He no longer chided me after that!)*

I then went on to explain that although I was not happy about the fact that the United States had the *'death penalty'* … since we're (supposedly) a Christian country and since we are not following the *teachings* of Christ, we're contradicting ourselves! The *death penalty* is proof of it.

It was at this point that the *five-minute warning bell* sounded, letting us know that class time would soon be ending. I gather up my class materials and walked to the door, opened it and waited.

Typically, the inmates would then gather together ... a distance of about 6' … to the right of where I stood.

Outside, in the hallway, the guard informed me that there might be a longer wait and he continued to remain in the hallway, just outside the door.

One of the inmates who identified himself as a Muslim said that he had "always understood that Christians believed in the Old Testament and that the Law of Moses – *'an eye for an eye'* – was also the Law of Mohammed."

I asked him if he knew the story of the *crucifixion* and he replied, "No." And at precisely that same moment, a mouse appeared from under the open door and stood up on its' hind legs and looked at me. I looked down at the mouse and said, "Would you also like to hear the story of the crucifixion?" *(Not only the inmates but the guard also witnessed the head of the mouse nod affirmatively!)*

I proceeded to tell the story, looking directly at the mouse and never looking up at the inmates.

I told how the man on the cross next to *Christ* knew that *Christ* could perform miracles and that he asked that he be released from the cross because he knew *Christ* had the power to do it. The other man, on the opposite cross recognized *Christ* as a *holy man* also and responded, "You have no right to ask for such a miracle because you and I are being punished because we're the ones who are guilty. He is a *holy man* is not guilty of anything and yet he's capable of forgiving those who are doing this thing to him."

Christ responded, "this day, you will be with me when I go to my Father in Heaven."

I then explained to the mouse that because most of *Christ's teachings* were about *forgiveness* and that everyone must "forgive their enemies" ... that his being crucified was the only way he could prove that he must do it!

When I told the mouse, "that is the end of the story," he went down on all fours and walked out into the hallway, past the guard who – like the inmates – had witnessed the episode, as well as heard the story I'd told the mouse.

Later, during the general business meeting which always followed classes, the same inmate who'd asked for the explanation of the "'crucifixion" told me that he "and the other Muslims believed the story."

When I asked him, "how can you be sure the story was true?" He replied, "what convinced all of us that the story was true was because of the appearance of the mouse and then the manner of how the mouse showed he was listening."

Truly, spirit moves in mysterious ways ... and this is an example of just that!

ARRIVING AT THE NICK-OF-TIME

One of my dearest friends whom I've known since we were both under the age of ten, was in her late 30's when this happened: I was working up in the Lake George Region at the time. I wasn't planning to make the drive back to Auburn that weekend but something – intuitively – told me to head back and that I needed to go directly to where she lived.

As I pulled up in her driveway, she was just stepping out the door of her house. When she looked up and saw me, she stood 'frozen'. I stepped out of my car and walked up to her.

Her face was pale, she smelled of booze and she was also shaking. "I can't believe you just came ... I was heading out the door to commit suicide!" she told me, tears streaming down her cheeks. Of course I stayed with her the entire weekend.

On Monday morning she went into *'rehab'* to deal with her drug and alcohol addiction.

After her recovery, she did a notable thing! She took the required training which – in time – enabled her to become licensed by the State of Pennsylvania to do 'cross-addiction counseling'. *(She became one of the best at it, working in one of this nation's 'best' rehab facilities where only those who were 'former addicts' are the counselors!)*

WHEN A GRANDMOTHER IS NEEDED MOST

Being present at the birth of my grandson, Christopher, is another story of *'help received from my angels'* ... because without them, he would not have lived!

As soon as he made his entrance into the world, I recognized that his condition was not good and I also saw the concerned look on the doctor's face. Christopher was immediately taken out of the delivery room ... and I followed.

During the over an hour that I stood beside the basket they'd laid him in, his left hand stayed tightly wrapped around the index finger of my right hand. I felt so helpless because there was nothing I could do for him ... except to say to myself, over and over again ... *"om, mani padme hom."*

I was well aware from the expressions on the faces of the medical staff that the baby's situation was tenuous. Both the doctor and nurses were checking on him every few minutes or so.

When the doctor finally spoke, he told me that he *"would have to take another course of action if things didn't improve for the baby within the next five minutes."* I knew then that prayer was all that I could do and so I prayed!

I immediately became aware of an unseen presence! Though I could not see the *'entity'*, I was certain it was there. I then noticed a change in the baby's breathing and also saw the baby's body relax. Then ... the sensed *'entity'* was gone!

When the doctor returned with the nurse and saw the change, his remark had a surprised tone to it, *"there's been a complete turn-around with this baby!"* A look of puzzlement came across his face as he looked at the monitor, "I don't understand what's happened here." He then bent over to listen to the baby's heart through his stethoscope. He then looked up at me, smiling, "I think he's going to be OK."

A SNAKE CAUSED LEVITATION TO OCCUR

This goes back to when I was first married to husband #1 in 1956. He liked to fish and on my first *fishing expedition* with him in Georgia, he took me to the Withlacoochee River.

We walked along a very narrow path beside the river, at the base of a 30 ft. high embankment. He tossed the line out into the murky water. His instructions were to hold the pole still and if I had 'a bite', I was to "snap it back and reel it in." *(He then proceeded back to the position he'd just left, upstream.)*

And so I waited. I mostly 'day-dreamed' during the several minutes I did wait. It was during those moments of day-dreaming that I was totally unaware of what was swimming toward me. When I finally did look down, I saw the head of a water moccasin only a few inches from my right foot! The next thing I recall was my husband standing beside me at the top of the embankment, shaking me and shouting! "What's wrong? What happened?"

When I finally came out of what might have been 'a state of shock' that must have lasted several minutes, I told him I'd "seen a snake!"

He couldn't understand how I'd gotten up to the top of the embankment. *(He had returned to see how things were going with my fishing and when finding me not there, looked up and saw me standing at the top of the embankment ... but was even more puzzled because he said, he "didn't see any 'scurry' marks up the embankment!")*

"You could not have gotten by me without my knowing it," he said, "and climbing up that embankment is the only other way you could have gotten up here."

And, even to this day I can only explain it as having been *'levitated'* by some external force or by my having 'levitated' myself! *(A number of other occurrences of levitation later occurred in my lifetime ... but I still don't know what did it or how I did it!)*

THE 'SPIRIT' OF TED CASE IN THE ATTIC

It was in late Spring of 1944 when I met Mr. Case. I was almost ten years old when I encountered him – *as a 'spirit'* – in the attic of the house I was living in at 9 Elizabeth Street in Auburn.

And, although our conversation was brief, I still recall his face and what he said. It was many years later before I came to know who he was. Nevertheless, because of the unbelievable circumstances under which we met ... our meeting is worth the telling!

It was in the late summer of 1975 that Professor Long, the museum's director, telephoned me. He asked me to stop by the museum because he had 'a project' he wanted me to get involved with. *(We worked together as board members on the Cayuga County Arts Council.)*

"A documentary film on the life of Theodore Case is to be done in Auburn and volunteer help is needed," he told me. When he asked if I'd help, I responded, "yes." *(It had been thirty years since I'd heard the name ... Theodore Case!)*

As I was sitting in front of Professor Long, learning for the first time about this Auburn native, he told me that "the building we're in was his home?" *(This was something I did not know ... nor did I know at that time that Mr. Case had been the inventor of 'talking pictures'. And, needless to say, I was amazed by what I was being told ... but had already been told by the 'spirit' I'd met in the attic of the house I lived in when I was 9 ½ yrs. old! And more about that will be revealed below!)* And, needless to say, I didn't let Professor Long know about my meeting Mr. Case! I recognized my own state of bewilderment about why this opportunity was being offered me at the time and what might be its connection with my meeting him in the attic of the house at 9 Elizabeth Street when I was very young.

I left the museum and because I had some time before my next appointment, I decided to go for a short drive and find a place to sit down and think about all that what was rattling around in my head ... hoping I could make some sense of it!

I don't know why the thought of going up to Fort Hill Cemetery – to see *Logan's Monument* – popped into my head at that moment ... but it did. *(I'd never seen it before!)*

I headed my car toward the cemetery, knowing I'd easily spot the obelisk at the highest point on the burial grounds.

After entering the side gate on Fort Street, the winding road continued upward. As I neared the top, I saw the obelisk to my right and so, pulled over … parking the car on the left side of the road.

As I stepped out of my car, I suddenly realized that the large family plot I had just parked next to belonged to the CASE FAMILY. *(And that added even further bewilderment to what I was already in the midst of experiencing!)* And, I don't know why I did it but I walked straight ahead and didn't stop until I reached the gravestone at the rear of the plot and only then did I look down. It was Theodore Case's headstone!

And when I looked up, off in the distance I could see the museum below ... Ted Case's childhood home.

(Since I did become the film's production supervisor, I have in my possession a scrapbook of photos and clippings about the filming. Local news media coverage was extensive during the time the film crew was in Auburn.)

The November 16, 1975 article which appeared in the local newspaper, *"Film Pioneer's Work Studied"* has photos which show members of the film crew, as well as pictures of both Professor Long and myself.

Working side-by-side with the Director Don L. Brodie was a most rewarding experience for me. I was especially pleased that he used my idea for the opening of the film ... showing Theodore Case's gravestone and then having the camera raise upward, zooming in on the door of the museum below. What followed next was George Kerstetter – *portraying Ted Case* – walking out the museum's front door.

Mr. Brodie shared many interesting stories about people he had worked with throughout his career in the film industry. His most amusing story was having to play the part of *"the first drag queen in Hollywood."* He went on to explain that he was actually hired by Walt Disney to dress in a witch's costume and then pose so that drawings could be done of him as the witch in the animated movie, *"Snow White."*

+ + + + + +

Years later, I worked as a 'docent' at the museum and at times I would recall having played the part of Mrs. Fox in the documentary filmed there. *(I also recalled having played my first piano recital in that same building at the age of five. The name of the piece was "The Twilight Song.")*

Another interesting 'tidbit' is that the museum houses a large piece of furniture – a buffet. According to the museum director, "they have no knowledge of who donated it." Well, what makes it particularly interesting to me is that it was once in my mother's home at 66 South Street. I know the piece well because I dusted it many times and recognized a watermark that's still on it! It's a piece of furniture she'd acquired at an 'auction' held in the Case mansion on South Street, back in the late 40's.

I also learned from George Kerstetter *(he played the role of Ted Case in the documentary film)* that, "Ted Case's wife grew up in the house at 9 Elizabeth Street." George also told me that "they were married in that same house."

(Now I could understand why Mr. Case was in the attic of the house I was living in. He was apparently visiting places he'd known while he was alive! It's something those who pass on can do ... after going to the other side.)

THE WORD 'AWED' EXPOSED A PRIEST!

Names are sometimes changed to protect both the guilty and the innocent. However, a wee bit of investigating could identify the people involved.)

My parapsychology group met a newcomer – a priest – the night we covered the topic of '*Reincarnation*'.

When we looked up and saw someone dressed as a priest, we thought things might go amiss! Though the public was always invited to our monthly meetings, we certainly never expected a priest to show up!

During Janice Munger's 'talk' on the topic she'd researched, the priest never spoke a word. He just sat and listened. However, at the conclusion, when she asked for 'input', he spoke up.

We were all surprised to hear about 'The Council of the Nicea' that had taken place during the Third Century. "It was at that Council," the priest said, "that the belief in 'reincarnation' was taken out of the Catholic Church." (None of us had ever heard that!)

> *(Of course that was in 1973 but today one only has to do a 'goggle' search and it is possible for the reader to type in ... "The Council of Nicea" ... and the proof is there that confirms it!)*

We were also surprised to also hear that many priests do *(privately)* believe in reincarnation. "After all," he told us, "how else do you 'reap what you sow'?"

After that meeting, the priest and I would frequently get together. He told me he'd "been a holy person in a previous lifetime." He also told me I'd "been a 'holy person' and that we'd been together at that same time."

(Despite his insistence, I had my doubts about what he was saying since I still found the belief in reincarnation the most difficult concept to accept.)

I was surprised that he admitted to me that he'd "recently had a child by a respectable woman in Auburn" who he named and who I also knew well. *(To this day she does not know that I know. The secret will go with me to the grave!)*

His broken English was sometimes difficult to understand and he would often ask me to define a word I'd used. For example: I'd used the word *"awed"* in a conversation with him one time and he asked me to explain its meaning ... which I did.

He sometimes boasted about the 'dissertation' he had written to obtain his doctoral degree. I was curious about it and so I asked if I could read it and he obliged by letting me borrow it that following week.

Coincidentally, my reading his dissertation came on the same week that Reverend Mae – my spiritual teacher – had asked me to do a 'vigil' to a saint, "any saint," she told us. I responded that "not having been raised a Catholic, I didn't feel compelled to do it" and she replied, "don't you want to find out if there's any credibility as to their existence?"

It was because of my doubts about this priest that I decided I'd ask St. Francis to answer my request. After all, since the priest was in the Franciscan Order, it seemed obvious I should do the 'vigil' to Saint Francis. (After 'lighting a candle', I read what I was instructed to and then asked the saint to "give me a sign whether or not to trust this priest?")

I recall well the night I decided to read the dissertation. It was after returning from driving the priest to a town near Rochester where he regularly performed an evening Mass. *(He had 'night blindness' and because of it, I often took turns with others to make the drive over and back for him.)*

After I started-up a fire in the fireplace, I took a bath and then got into my flannel pajamas. I pickcd up the copy of his *dissertation* that I had laid down on the night stand next to my bed and headed back to the couch in my living room. En-route, a picture dropped out of the manuscript. When I picked it up, I recognized it as the picture of *'The Infant of Prague'*. *(I took it as 'a confirming sign' that my answer might be within the pages of the dissertation.)*

I laid the manuscript on my lap ... closed my eyes and asked *spirit* to "help me locate the page on which an 'answer' might be found." There followed a loud 'pop' and I opened my eyes to see that the fireplace had suddenly gone out! *(Prior to closing my eyes ... it had been a blazing fire! I was also aware of a 'spirit' presence! And so, closed my eyes again ... and waited.)*

Several seconds went by. I continued to wait, silently saying the words which Reverend Mae had said we should say during any 'waiting' period for a response. I soon became aware of pages being turned ... and then it stopped! I raised my right arm and with my index finger extended, I became aware of something pressing against the top of my hand, pushing it downward until my finger tip touched the page. I opened my eyes and the word I pointed to was the word, **awed**!

"How could he have written this dissertation?" I asked myself. "He's used the word 'awed' in it and yet, had just asked me that day 'the definition of it' because he did not know its' meaning." And then, a super-imposed picture began to build before me, filling the front of the entire

room. I was seeing the priest and he was handing a young man six one hundred dollar bills. I instinctively knew it was the young man who'd actually written the work and the priest was paying him for his efforts!

The next morning I called the rectory and informed the secretary that I "would be stopping by and dropping off something for the priest?"

After ringing the door bell at the rectory's side door, it was the priest who opened the door. When he saw the dissertation in my hands, he led me to an adjoining room. I then proceeded to tell him of the previous night's vision.

He immediately became 'unglued' and accused me of being a *witch*! He ordered me to leave!

That same week, I went to see another member of the Franciscan Order … a priest who held a higher position in the Order. Although I didn't tell him what I had learned about the dissertation, I did make reference to the priest's questionable association with a woman … who I was certain was becoming that priest's next victim.

The priest immediately began verbally assaulting me by accusing me of "having seduced the priest by committing a horrible sin and turning the young priest away from the vocational path he'd been on!" *(The older priest would never have accepted the truth of how I'd actually become the young priest's 'confessor' and that I had not made him my victim!)*

(No doubt the numerous messages I'd been giving the 'guilty' priest had somehow convinced him that I could be his

*'personal confessor' ... having already telling me about his
'affair' and the woman who had "given birth to his child."
But this I withheld from the older priest because I did not
want to expose the truth of who the young priest's first victim
really was ... a woman who was a member of the same
church, who had a high-standing in the community, as did
the priest's newest victim whose deceased husband was also
known by the older priest! And, to-date, I've kept the secret!)*

What I did know was that the older priest was familiar with
the young priest's newest victim because he'd converted her
to Catholicism prior to her marriage to a man within his own
church. He'd also later baptized the couple's baby. And
then, a few years later, conducted the funeral Mass for her
husband who'd been killed tragically. Thus, when I told the
older priest who the new victim was ... he reacted, as I was
sure he would!

The end result of the investigation was that the young priest
had to leave the priesthood and marry the woman who – *to
this day* – still believes that he left the priesthood because he
loved her!

A POST OFFICE BOX ABOVE THE BAPTISM FONT

I attended the First Baptist Church when I grew up in
Auburn. It was located on the corner of James and Genesee
Streets. It was because the walls of the building were
deteriorating that the building was torn down in the 70's to
make room for the new post office building. I had a post
office box there and it was where I received all my mail.

When I finally made the decision to be ordained, it was later
that I received my ordination papers in that post office box.

128

POSSIBILITIES

It was while I stood there, looking at the *Certificate of Ordination* that I suddenly realized that I was standing over the exact location where the church's baptism font had been. *(I was baptized in it at the age of 12, as was my twin sister.)* "Funny," I thought "I hadn't thought about that fact before that moment!" It was the 'irony' of standing over the spot that I suddenly experienced *'a rapt in awe'* moment!

It was much later I realized that it was in a *past life (as a monk)* that I'd believed what was then a *'doctrine of the church'* that *"no woman could be a member of the clergy"* and because this was a belief at the time that was not correct, I would have to return in a future life to unlearn a *'false'* belief and find that it was <u>instead</u> ... acceptable to be clergy.

WILLIAM SMITH WAS A SPIRITUALIST

My getting the job of 'executive director' of the <u>Finger Lakes Arts Council</u> in 1982 was no accident either! *(At the time I got the offer, I was working as the executive director of the Lower Adirondack Regional Arts Council where I'd successfully expanded their annual arts and crafts festival from an 8,000 attendance to over 20,000 attendees.)*

The board of directors of the <u>Finger Lakes Arts Council</u> (FLAC) had purchased the Geneva Theater and wanted to restore it to its' original grandeur and it was my job to begin the restoration process.

After coming to the job, I found out that it had originally been built as an opera house in 1894 and that it had opened with James O'Neil – father of Eugene O'Neil – playing the role of the Count of Monte Cristo. Many 'greats' also appeared on the stage of the Smith Opera House that

included Ellen Terry who was considered the 'greatest
Shakespearean performer' of her day ... who I had known!

Shortly after coming on board of the FLAC, I decided that
I'd do a *'psychic fair'* as a fund raiser and so I proceeded
down to speak with the editor of the local newspaper – *The_*
Finger Lakes Times about the idea. He promptly told me,
"not to expect the newspaper to give any publicity on that
kind of thing!" He then added, *"We won't even let you place*
any paid advertising in the newspaper about it either!"

When I left the building, I walked on up the hill to the
historical society's building where I asked the secretary if I
might take a look at the 'opera house' files.

There were several file boxes. I'd already been told, "none
of the boxes were in any order." I opened the file box
closest to me. I began at the front and did a quick scan of
each piece of paper that I was pulling out and putting back,
making a mental note of what I was looking at. I saw a
programs, one or two payroll records, a candy order voucher,
a number of old newspaper clippings, etc.

But I also began noticing one piece of paper that was near
the back of the box which appeared to be slowly moving
upward. *(Because I sensed it might be being moved by*
'spirit', I sat back and waited. Sure enough ... it continued
its upward movement.)

The paper appeared to be official in nature and when I read
what it said, that "William Smith was a Spiritualist." *(You*
can imagine my excitement!) I took it to the society's
secretary who made a copy of the paper, acknowledging on
it that it was "a copy of a *document* in their archives."

I returned to the newspaper office and walked into the editor's office and handed him the *document.* After reading it, he looked up and said, *"Well I guess you'll get your feature article in The Finger Lakes Times after all!"*

And so, the next day's newspaper 'feature article' opened with the following words: "If William Smith were alive today he would most certainly attend this weekend's psychic fair at the Smith Opera House."

PLAYING A ROLE IN "THE BAD SEED"

While at the Smith Opera House I was offered a part in the local community theater's play, *"The Bad Seed." (I was not familiar with either the play nor the book.)* However, as I read through the lines I realized that one of my own children was without a doubt … also *'a bad seed'*!

It is because of the continuing situation that exists that I am not able to elaborate on what one of my own children has been doing throughout their lifetime. But, let me give you one small bit of insight about that child which I wrote about in a *'letter to the editor'* that was published on 12/12/03 in the Auburn newspaper: *The Citizen.* It will provide the reader the needed insight of why I call my child *'a bad seed'.*

The letter is titled: *"Foster family needs to know truth about my child!"*

(My letter was in response to someone else who had written a letter the previous week about their dissatisfaction with the local Child Protective Services.)

Basically my letter explained what had happened in my own

situation ... that my teen ager partied one summer night with some of her friends in the local cemetery ... *without my permission.*

The child came home that evening under the influence of alcohol/drugs ... with several visible injuries to the face, arms and legs ... due to having had an accident on a borrowed mini-bike. The child was hysterical and my efforts to calm the child down were futile. We got into a scuffle but I was able to contain all efforts to hurt me. Finally, I did something I'd never done before ... I slapped the child across the face! Startled by it, the child left the house and never returned that night." *(But not coming home at night had become 'a recent regular habit'!)*

"The next morning I had a phone call from Child Protective Services requesting that I come to their office as soon as I could. I was told that I was being charged with 'physical child abuse'."

"After leaving the house, my child had fled to a friend's home where upon entering the parents saw the outward appearance of the child and assumed that the child had been beaten. When they asked what had happened, the answer given was, 'My mother hit me.' They took the child to the emergency room at Auburn Memorial Hospital. And, the next day I was charged with 'child abuse'!"

When I was later questioned by the head of the Child Protective Agency, all I knew was that "the injuries sustained were due to having crashed themselves on a borrowed minibike."

Later I learned from neighbor kids who were there that night that the accident had occurred at the cemetery. What they told me was "the headlight went out and the mini-bike crashed into one of the tombstones."

My letter continued: "And it was what the neighbor kids had told me that I reported back to Child Protective Services and in time, they were able to verify the validity of my story and I was absolved of the charge."

Nevertheless, it was mutually agreed that the child remain in the foster home.

While living in the foster home, there was never a problem for the family or at school ... behavior was cited as being 'favorable/commendable'. Two years later, my child graduated with honors.

My letter ended with: "So here's my contention with Child Protective Services! They never told the foster home family, before nor after the child left their care that I was not guilty of the abuse charge, nor were they told the reasons why CPS felt there was a need for the child to remain with them."

"... I feel justified telling my story because even though God knows the truth, sometimes others need to know the truth also – especially the foster family who most needs to read this letter and hopefully they will."

And if this isn't enough, over the years I have had to encounter the wrath of some who still believe it to be so! **(*)**

(I later learned from a credible source that the couple did read the letter in the newspaper and told the source that they

agreed that Social Services should have told them.")

(*) *Let me relate one such incident of returned 'wrath' ... by the mother of one of the girls my child graduated with. The woman was a nurse at Auburn Memorial Hospital. When I was brought up to her floor – after surgery for a broken tibia-plateau to my right leg – she delayed giving me my medication for pain. When she entered the room, she closed the door behind her. No one else was in the other bed. We were alone. I instinctively knew she was going to hurt me! She slammed me up against the railing as hard as she could and while doing so said, "I'm doing this because of what you did to your child, you evil bitch." Fortunately, I passed out!*

The next thing I knew I was being taken down to Intensive Care where I remained for a whole week. And, although I later reported the incident to the hospital's head administrator, he did nothing.

ASHLEY'S BELIEF IN THE 'LITTLE PEOPLE'

None of my other children saw *spirits* but Ashley did ... till he was around the age of 12. It was the *'little people'* he most enjoyed seeing. He would leave notes for them ... attached to the base of the large maple tree in the back yard.

I recall one episode when we were living in Castle Rock, Pennsylvania. He called to me to come outside and when I opened the back door, he pointed to one of the trees. *"Look, mom ... the little people are on the lowest branch and they're going to jump up and down on it."* And, sure enough, the branch began to go up and down. I also noticed there was no breeze stirring. *(However, because I was aware that there were three other brothers who might be well hidden who were also participating in this 'demonstration' and had a rope tied to the branch.)* That I then asked Ashley, "Can the little people go to that branch – pointing to another tree, several trees over – and jump up and down on it?"

Much to my surprise the branch on the tree I'd pointed at began to go up and down!

Ashley often shared with me his experiences of seeing 'spirit'. He was never afraid of them. He never shared anything bizarre. And, although he believed in evil entities, he told me that he knew he was "protected from them."

(I know he was a 'gifted child' and a doctor at Stanford University told me so. I don't recall the doctor's name but he was conducting a state-wide study of 'gifted and talented children' in the State of California during the late 60's. The test the doctor was administering "provided him with that proof," he said.)

THE LOSS OF A SON – HIS SUICIDE

In November, 2005, as a result of a local newspaper story about 'bullying in the schools', I decided to write a letter to the editor. It appeared in <u>The Citizen's</u> (11/22/05) issue:

"Reading the first-hand accounts of local students who shared their stories about being homosexual made me realize how far we've come since the mid-70's when I learned that my own 15 year old son was 'gay'.

"(The public's attitude was even tougher on a kid who was 'gay' back then!)

"An 'A' student, Ashley was frequently bullied in school by students. *(On one occasion, several boys attacked him in the school yard during the lunch hour and he sustained a broken arm. Nothing was ever done about it by the school's administration.) Ultimately, my son quit school because of the continuing harassment.*

"He went to live with his father in the State of Washington. During the year he was there, he 'came out'! That upset his dad and he was 'kicked out'.

"I pleaded with my son to come home instead but he'd already made up his mind to go to San Francisco, "where 'gays' can openly live on the streets," he told me.

"A year later, he returned to Auburn. (The abuse 'gays' were exposed to at that time was also horrendous in the City of Auburn ... even by some of the local police officers..)

"Shortly after his return, I discovered a letter he'd written to a friend. In it he said, he "was planning to commit suicide." When I asked him about what he'd written, he said, "it's the reason I came back ... I want to be able to do it here."

"Despite my pleading, he repeated the words over and over again, 'Mom my mind is made up. I plan to do it.' To appease me, he finally agreed to talk to a psychologist.

"I spoke to a friend, a child psychologist who held a prominent position in the city at that time. He agreed to talk to Ashley.

"I can assure you, your son won't do it," I was told. (I also talked to two other professionals in the mental health field and both concurred with what the child psychologist had told me.)"

Unfortunately they were all wrong! He committed suicide.

It was several years after his suicide that I was finally able to go through his personal effects, also his writings. I learned what I should have been aware of ... but I was blind to it. Truly, what happens in a home is so often missed! But what he'd written gave me the knowledge of why he was so upset with his dad for 'kicking him out'.

THE SHIP ON THE SEA OF GALILEE

Prior to the death of my son, I was convinced that there was nothing that would <u>ever</u> cause me to lose my faith. <u>But I did lose it that day</u>! And, when I went to bed that night ... an unusual thing happened! *(It was the second time I'd experienced the 'building' of a super-imposed picture in the room!)*

The *scene* before me was clearly visible and one that I immediately recognized! It was the scene described in the *Bible* of the ship on the *Sea of Galilee* being tossed about because of the storm!

Visible to me in the scene before me were the disciples and they were panicking, convinced they were doomed! I saw Thomas going down into the hull and waking Jesus up. *"Wake up Master, there's a storm and we're all going to die!"* Christ' replied, *"No, it won't happen because my*

Father knows where I am."

Christ came up on deck, raised his arms and as he did so, the storm subsided. Thomas responded by saying, *"The storm was probably going to end anyway, right?"* Christ chided him by saying, *"Thomas you always doubt me."* And then I witnessed Jesus stepping over the side of the boat ... he walked on the water!

I immediately knew the *'lesson'* of the dramatization I'd just witnessed and my *faith* was immediately restored!

(It's because his disciples could witness his miracles and still lose their faith that it was also OK for me to lose mine! By losing my faith, it was also a way of being 'tested' ... letting me know that my faith wasn't as strong as it needed to be!)

THE RACHEL CARSON POSTAGE STAMP

When I walked into the public library in Glens Falls one day, I glanced over to the table where the most recent books acquired by the library were on exhibit. I was surprised to see Dr. Rachel Carson's book, *"Silent Spring"* among them. *(I was surprised because her book had already come out in the late 1960's and in my own mind I questioned why it would be appearing on the table with 'new releases'!)*

Nevertheless, I decided to pick the book up because I had always intended to read it. As I stood in the check-out line waiting to take the book out, I happened to open it to the page where the word *"dieldrin"* appeared at the top of the page. I read the paragraph describing it. *"It is the chemical used by landscapers and then it was subsequently banned because of its mind-altering side effects', including episodes of mania"* ... and <u>I immediately knew I'd found the underlying cause of Jim's unexplained 'episodes of mania</u>'!

After I checked out the book, I made copies of the pages of that chapter on the library's copier.

I immediately drove to the post office and asked for a stamped, legal-sized envelope and inserted the copied pages. After sealing the envelope, I addressed it to Jim at Auburn prison.

I knew the weight of the several pages would mean additional postage and so asked the clerk to check the weight and let me know whether more postage was needed? She said "it requires an additional 14 cent stamp." She passed the stamp to me.

Much to my surprise the stamp had Dr. Carson's picture on it! *(Here was a 'confirming sign' that this was indeed Jim's answer and I also realized that 'spirit' was helping.)*

I asked the clerk when they'd gotten the new stamps and she replied, "the stamps came in today."

When I saw Jim on my next trip back to Auburn, he 'thanked' me for my letter because he now had an answer to the unexplained 'episodes' he'd been having over the several years he'd been doing landscaping. *(One such 'episode' occurred during the commission of his crime.)*

(The 'episodes' stopped a year after he came into prison. According to Dr. Carson, "they would stop but only if the

*chemical wasn't being handled any longer." As the reader
may know, she was the recipient of the Nobel Prize in
Chemistry!)*

Unfortunately the state has never considered the 'mitigating circumstances' in his case!

A CONNECTION TO A NEIGHBOR'S CRISIS

I was invited to 'speak' at one of the local VFW's in Auburn.
Over seventy-five people were in attendance. (*Spirit was a
big help to me that night*.) I picked up on many in
attendance and provided correct information on each. I was
also able to confirm the health issues of one of the attendees'
loved ones. *(I used my dowsing rod to illustrate how it was
possible to 'lock in' on the imaginary body to confirm what
the existing problems was with that person's loved one
because the antenna would 'stop' at certain places on what
was an unseen body.)*

People were asked to make a donation and a collection plate
was passed around. At the end of the 'demonstration' I
handed the collection plate to the individual who had invited
me to come that evening … donating back the money to
their organization.

Approximately a month later one of the attendees phoned
me and asked if I'd "help with finding a missing relative?"
Her uncle's small plane – headed to Syracuse from North
Carolina – "had disappeared and where had it gone down?"

My response to her was the usual one. *(I would need "to go
to church and ask for a 'sign' to confirm that 'spirit' would*

give the help needed.")

I went to St. Mary's church and knelt at the foot of the statue
of the Blessed Mother. During the praying I became aware
of a light-touching-feeling on my folded hands. When I
opened my eyes, rose petals had fallen from the roses that
were being held in the statue's hands. Three landed on my
hands/none on the floor. This was a 'sign' that help would be
given!

What followed was a significant discomfort on my right side
and ... *an awareness that a kidney was missing'!*

When I phoned the girl who'd called for 'help' and asked
about 'a missing kidney'? She responded that the *missing*
uncle had given one of his kidneys to a son!

My response to her was that "in three days the plane will be
discovered by men out hunting." And, three days later,
despite a heavy snow storm, the plane was found by men
hunting. I was also told that "despite a heavy snow storm
the night before, the crashed plane was laid bare ... not a
flake of snow on it! *(Unfortunately her uncle had been
killed in the crash.)*

The young caller 'thanked' me and said that her mother
"would like to meet me." A weekday morning time was
agreed upon since her mother "would be coming into
Auburn that day."

The girl's mother showed up and I escorted her into the
conference room where I worked in the Metcalf building.
She 'thanked' me for the 'message' given to her daughter

about her missing brother and it was "knowing he would be found" that she said, "comforted" her. *(She also admitted that she realized that "since the plane was missing ... the likelihood would be that he was killed in the crash.")*

We prayed together. And, because I sensed the presence of *spirit,* I told her so. "It's the person whose apron you were wearing this morning." She replied, "it was my mom's apron I had on." What came to me next was her 'finding an earring in the pocket of the apron' and I told her so. Her immediate response, "yes, it's an earring that's been missing for years!" *(Thus 'proof' her mother was there with us!)* A period of 'silence' followed so she could close her eyes and communicate with her 'loved one'.

It was agreed that I "should come do a 'circle' for family and friends" and a date and time were agreed upon.

It was 7 pm when I arrived at the family home and a group of twenty-five were gathered together in the large living room. I soon discovered that the people included not only the family members but several people who attended their church in Scipioville.

(Whenever I've done a 'circle' ... it is understood that I not be given the names of those who will attend. I've also made it a habit to be sure the host/hostess be a person who has 'credibility' ... a person that will never share information about any of the 'guests'. There are no introductions when I arrive, although I usually begin by saying: "Thank you for coming. Your host/hostess has told me all about you ..." (and there's usually a bit of laughter at this point!) Those attending are instructed "do not consume any alcohol

prior to attending.")

The help from *spirit* was greatly evident … most everyone there received a *'message'* … but one person in particular was getting more than the usual number of them! Finally I turned to the man and blurted out, "you've just returned from an out-of-town trip where you had an interview for a job!" He stood up, looked around the room and speaking to the group said, "not one of you in this room knew that I'd gone out of town and I had no intention of telling you till Sunday when you come to church to hear the announcement that I'm probably going to accept that job." He then turned to me and said, "I am convinced – for the first time – that you are definitely communicating with those on the *other side* and I want to invite you to my church this Sunday so that I can acknowledge what I've witnessed here this evening."

On that following Sunday I did attend h the minister's church in the village of Scipioville … and he acknowledged me and what I had done … saying that I'd "proved that we can communication with our loved ones."

It was also the church Mr. Ward had only ever attended from early childhood and where his 'memorial service' was conducted at the time of his demise. He is buried in the cemetery ½ mile up the road. It is his name I mentioned on the 'DEDICATION' page of this book. *(He was like a grandfather to me from the age of two to the age of ten when my mother broke up with him … however, she forbid my ever seeing him again!)* But she did (reluctantly) give me permission to see him in his coffin in 1950 at the Brew Funeral Home.

+ + + + + + + + + + + + + + +

THE PLAY – "BLITHE SPIRIT"

Shortly after returning to Auburn, I got involved with the Auburn Community Players group … auditioning for a part in a play being directed by Sam Kennedy *(editor of the local newspaper)*.   After auditioning for the first play he wanted to do, he decided to do another play, *"Blithe Spirit"* by Noel Coward and I was given the part of "Madame Arcadi" – the 'flaky' medium. *(At the time, no one knew I was heavily involved in parapsychology.)*

(It is important to mention also that 'memorizing' was always a very difficult feat for me … perhaps it had something to do with my dyslexia; nevertheless, I was determined to learn the part!)

Despite the fact that I was a *novice … everyone else having had extensive training and/or experience in the field of theater …*it was I who received the *'standing ovation'* by a packed house of professionals that attended the show.

(The following 'excerpts' are taken from the news article that appeared in The Citizen on: Sunday, November 20, 1971:

"The ladies in long formal gowns, and in fashion's latest formal pant dresses, escorted by gentlemen in "black tie" formal wear entered in large talkative groups and began to exchange light talk in the hall and lounge of the Union …
… it was the last event to be held in the soon to be demolished Osborne Hall.

"The lights flashed, curtain opened and Mary Taylor and Lou Ryan as Ruth and Charles began their anxious

preparation for the arrival of medium Madame Arcati (Joyce Hackett) who suited the part perfectly ...

"You had to be there to appreciate the well-spoken, excellently timed lines so expertly loaded with punch, wit, and humor as Noel Coward wrote them. Gestures and attitude, as well as a put-on crackly voice made by Joyce Hackett the scene stealer, as an incredibly spirited, bouncy and ambitious practitioner of the occult. She once said she must be "on to work," but "play" would have been more like it. Not the stereotyped fortune teller, she was instead a saucy quipper, full of smart comments and a firm believer in the riding of a bicycle to work. She was in command of the situation at all times, except in her numerous "out-cold" trance scenes."

(The mention of a real bat *'flying over actors on the stage'* during the séance scene was definitely *'a sign'* to me that there was some assistance from *'the other side'!)*

THE PLAY – "CIRCLES"

I wrote a play that was based on what a Chicago newspaper reporter witnessed and then reported in a series of articles in the 1880's. He attended several 'circles' and reported on the several witnessed 'paranormal events' that occurred and which he witnessed. *(See the last chapter: "Voices From The Grave" for the 'excerpts' that were used in the play 'Circles'.)*

The play *'Circles'* was directed by Bourke Kennedy *(co-founder of the Auburn Players Community Theater).* Several of the performers who donated their time held professional jobs in the community. Both nights of the show were sold-out!

AN AMERICAN ARTIST

Although the other LARAC board members considered my efforts in getting Loren Blackburn's art featured in <u>American Artist</u> magazine a *'feather in my cap'* … the <u>credit</u> really goes to my *'angels'* who helped make it possible!

(I know this because as I approached the Auriesville Shrine near Fonda, New York, I asked for 'a sign' that Loren's work would be accepted? The confirming 'sign' – a large red rose – appeared on the side of a tractor trailer truck which passed my window when I was directly opposite the site.)

Prior to leaving Glens Falls an hour earlier, I'd gotten several transparencies from him of his paintings and sent them to the *artistic director* of the magazine, by 'certified/return receipt mail' from the post office. And before the green card came back, Loren had already received a phone call from them saying, "we're going to feature your work in our magazine." And they did feature him in the March 1991 issue of their magazine on their *'Watercolor Pages'*.

The fact that Loren passed away as I was re-writing this chapter of my book … on June 16, 2017 … is another confirmation of their being aware of what I'm doing!)

Loren Blackburn held a white-collar position as marketing director for a top engineering firm in Albany, New York. His company had reproduced his art work on their calendar for years. Upon seeing the calendar, I asked Loren if I 'could promote his work' and he responded, "go right ahead!" *(But he said it with a grin on his face!)*

However, prior to this happening, there was a close call of my being 'fired' by Loren Blackburn ... because of a newspaper article!

I'd been asked by a fellow well-known dowser – Ted Kaufman – if I'd "volunteer my time to show 5th graders the *'art of dowsing'* at a Warren County BOCES annual 'outing'?" *(Other planned 'outdoor' demonstrations done by volunteers included: edible plant identification, astronomy, campfire building, first aid, etc.)*

I was not aware that day that a local newspaper photographer had taken my picture when I was standing in the midst of the students who were watching my dowsing demonstration. And, when the photo appeared in the next morning's newspaper with the caption: "A Water Witch Demonstration" ... I got a phone call from Loren Blackburn saying he "was very upset about the picture in the paper" and in a condescending tone then said, "I'm leaving to go to Toronto on business this morning but when I get back on Friday morning, I will be in to see you right after lunch!" *(At the time he was the President of the LARAC board.)*

It was only five minutes after 1 pm. when he walked into my office and in his hand, a copy of a magazine. He plopped down a U.S. Air magazine on the table before me ... saying, "This magazine happened to be in the back pocket of the seat in front of where I was seated and I want you to know, an article in it saved you your job!"

He opened the magazine to the article about the *'Danville Dowsers'. (These dowsers were able to prove their 'dowsing' abilities to the Massachusetts Institute of Technology!)*

He later acknowledged to the other members of the board of directors that I had called him before he received the phone call from American Artist about "being accepted in the magazine." He also acknowledged my having "mailed the transparencies off to the magazine prior to leaving Glens Falls and then getting a confirming *sign* when driving past the Auriesville Shrine en-route to Auburn."

'ROSARY' ON A LICENSE PLATE

It was common for others to also witness what I was a witness to! What follows is proof of it.

I was riding with my friend, Nancy Cheney and as we were coming down South Street, we were discussing in detail all that I'd been going through, as it relates to a 'troublesome landlord' who was getting away with what could only be construed as *'fraud'* ... when I made the following statement, *"The Boss knows what she's been doing and – in time – He'll deal with her!"*

The light was red as we pulled up behind a car in front of the city hall building and much to our surprise the license plate on the car directly ahead of us read: "ROSARY"! *(A confirming 'sign' that what I'd just said about THE BOSS handling the problem ...would surely happen!)*

THE SIGNS OF ST. FRANCIS

A series of seven *'signs'* related to Saint Francis occurred for a week, in conjunction with the incident written earlier in this Chapter about the priest who was exposed. *(Given the fact that the priest was a Franciscan priest ... I am convinced I may have actually had help from the Saint!)*

What follows is one of the more significant *signs*!

I arrived at my attorney's office and he asked me to "have a seat." When his phone rang, he answered it and indicated that I should remain. *(Not wanting to appear that I was listening, I got up from my chair and began taking a closer look at the art work on the walls of his office.)* One of the framed pictures really surprised me! It was an *abstract* etching of St. Francis.

After the lawyer completed his call, I pointed to the print and said, "I have to tell you that I never would have believed that a Jewish lawyer would have a rendering of Saint Francis hanging on his office wall."

The lawyer was emphatic with his response, "No it's not … it's an etching of a tree!" I replied, "Sorry Mike but it really is Saint Francis." *(He got up from his chair and came to take a closer look and recognizing what he really was seeing remarked, "you are right!")*

He promptly took the framed print off the wall and commenced to put it in the top drawer of his desk. I wanted it and asked, *"can I buy it?"* He said, *"of course you can"* and he turned the framed print over to reveal a sales tag of $13.00 dollars on it … and that is exactly what I paid for it!

(I later gave the framed print to my friend, Nancy Cheney. She's the real estate broker I mentioned in the previous 'story' because I'm convinced that in a past life, we were nuns in the Franciscan Order.)

The seven 'signs' of St. Francis that week convinced me

that there really are Saints and they're closest to the Boss!

AND SO, FORGIVING IS THE HARDEST TEST OF ALL!

A reminder that the *'mouse story'* in Chapter One tells the reader that *'forgiveness'* is what Christ was able to prove that he could do! To be willing for any of us to forgive someone who is 100% guilty of the *worst possible crime* would be impossible for most to do. However, passing the hardest tests of all is the reason we're here on Planet Earth and until we can do it ... we'll continue to come back again & again! *(Reincarnation is also referred to as: KARMA!)*

JUDAS WAS NOT A TRAITOR!

It has only been in recent years that the Catholic Church has finally acknowledged that Judas was not a traitor but instead, the messenger, doing what Christ asked him to do. After all, if His most important 'teaching' was 'forgiveness' ... then Judas clearly understood what he was being asked to do!

Of course we know that Jesus upset the rabbis because most of his 'teachings' contradicted what was Jewish law ... for example their law of *'an eye for an eye'*! *(A reminder that most Christians still subscribe to it. It's also the law of Muslims!)* Even Mark Twain chided about the 'law' ... saying: "Follow that 'law' and we'll all end up blind!"

In a later Chapter of this book the reader will come to understand that I was able to come to the realization that it was because of a *'past life'* that in this life, I would still have to 'forgive' someone who – *in a past life* – had killed me.

ANGEL IMPS
CARTOON CREATIONS

In the early 1990s, I began drawing cartoon caricatures of 'Angel Imps'. I thought of possible names which would match their name to what I drew. An illustration of many of them is shown below.

A decade later, I put all of them into a self-published small book and cited many of the *quotes* we've often heard throughout our lifetimes, I illustrated the Angel Imps ... repeating those familiar quotes. One of the chapters from the book is included herein. It is the story of Angel Angus who takes his young charge, Twinkle on a visit into a prison.

(Shown with Father Time are Angel Angus, Little Boo Peep, Twinkle, Hug-a-Boo, Scardy Cat, Peek-a-Boo, Snoop Spook and Silly Spook.)

Later that year, on May 8, 2010, I wrote a play and also wrote music to it. The *'Angel Imp'* characters performed with a 'known' character .. MARK TWAIN!

What follows is the PROGRAM:

╋ ╋ ╋ ╋ ╋ ╋ ╋ ╋ ╋ ╋ ╋ ╋ ╋ ╋

THE AUBURN PLAYERS COMMUNITY THEATRE'S

SECOND STAGE

PRESENTS

THE PREMIER OF THE MUSICAL COMEDY

WE'RE NO ANGELS ... WE'RE IMPS !

╋ ╋ ╋ ╋ ╋ ╋ ╋ ╋ ╋ ╋ ╋ ╋ ╋ ╋ ╋ ╋

STARRING ALAN CLUGSTON as MARK TWAIN

CREATED BY: JOYCE HACKETT SMITH

PRESS RELEASE

SECOND STAGE TO HOLD AUDITIONS

Auditions for the Auburn Players Community Theater's Second Stage will be held from 2 p.m. to 5 p.m., Saturday, February 27th at the United Ministry Church in Aurora.

Actors, age 8 and up, are needed for principal roles for "We're No Angels – We're Imps" – a newly created musical/comedy that will be premiered at the Morgan Opera House on Saturday, May 8th at 2 p.m. and 7 p.m.

It was only after the show's creator Joyce Hackett Smith was able to persuade Alan Clugston to play the role of Mark Twain that Bourke decided to produce the show as *readers' theater.*

Smith says that "although Mr. Twain believed in God, his satirical remarks – about how folks interpreted their religious beliefs – often got him in trouble! As a member of the clergy myself, I've witnessed the truth of much of what he wrote about in his book, 'Letters From This Earth'. Some of his 'truth', as well as my own, is revealed in the show. "

There are four musical numbers and auditionees should bring their own sheet music and be prepared to sing 16 measures of an up-tempo song. A solo dance number requires appropriate footwear for the audition.

The production is intended to bring attention to the needs of the Southern Cayuga Emergency Food Bank and food items will be requested instead of an admission price at the door.

Bourke Kennedy, of the Auburn Players' Second Stage, will direct the production and Ms. Siouxsie Grady, Chairman of the Wells College's Performing Arts Department, has offered to assist in several capacities.

WE'RE NO ANGELS ... WE'RE IMPS"

G. Alan Clugston . . . . Mark Twain

Alan Clugston, Emeritus Professor of English at Wells
College, has acted numerous times with the Auburn Players
Community Theatre, Merry-Go-Round Playhouse, Kitchen
Theatre, Syracuse University and Wells College. He has also
"Scrooged" around the Morgan Opera House. He lends his
voice to the Masterworks Chorale when not on stage with
area theatrics.

Mark Drabicki . . . . Joe & Ares

Mark Drabicki makes this third on stage appearance with
"Joe". He has been an active participant with the Auburn
Players Second Stage Original Short Play Festival.

Katie Moran . . . . Minister & Zeus

Katie Moran broke into the local theatre scene several years
ago with the Loose Ends Theater Group. She has played a
variety of parts from vampire hunter to President of the
U.S., from a Moliere maid to town sheriff.

Logan MacNicol . . . . Twinkle

Logan MacNicol is a 12 year old who is no stranger to the
stage. His first role was as Tiny Tim for Loose Ends
Theatre. Keep him away from good china though. ("I
accidentally broke the prop lady's china plate when I was
supposed to slam down my cup ... I cleaned it up.")

Anna Feldman . . . . Angie & Hera

Anna Feldman is a senior at Wells College, majoring in
English. She is a member of "Henry's VIII" and has been
in and directed "The Vagina Monologues". This is her
debut on the Morgan Opera House stage and she's thrilled
to be able to do this before she graduates!

154   POSSIBILITIES

Eden Kostick . . . . Prisoner

Eden Kostick is a senior Performing Arts major at Wells
College. She has choreographed and performed for many
shows in the past four years, including her senior thesis:
"Choreutic Harmony".

Crystal Rightmyer . . . . Scardy Cat/ Aphrodite

Crystal Rightmyer is a student at Wells College. She has
played a number of smaller roles in several college
productions. She has also been helpful behind the scenes as
well.

Ron VanNostrand . . . . Father Time

Ron VanNostrand has been a musical performer for 44
years. He has resided in Central New York for 25 years.
He was a columnist for a number of years for the Auburn
Citizen. He now enjoys writing and editing "Olive Trees", a
creative literary magazine ... since 1984.

MUSIC DIRECTOR: *Dan Williams is a music and theatre graduate
of SUNY Oswego. He is excited to be making his music directing debut
with the Second Stage. He is in demand as musical director or assistant
for area schools, most recently as assistant for "Seussical" in Cicero. As
an actor he has performed with Appleseed, Oswego Players and Port City.
(He 'thanks' his Aunt Joyce for giving him the opportunity to be the
Music Director.)*

THE AUBURN PLAYERS COMMUNITY THEATRE
SECOND STAGE
PRESENTS

WE'RE NO ANGELS ... WE'RE IMPS

WORDS & MUSIC BY: JOYCE HACKETT SMITH-MOORE
ADAPTED FOR STAGE BY: BOURKE KENNEDY

SATURDAY – MAY 8TH – 2 PM & 7 PM
MORGAN OPERA HOUSE

WE'RE NO ANGELS song by: *"Hugger Mugger"*

I'M NO ANGEL ...
       I AIN'T GOT WINGS
I DON'T DO MAGIC
              GRANTING WISHES ... JUST AIN'T MY THING!

WHAT I DO ... DO
              IS LOOK AND LISTEN ...
WATCHING ALL THE FOLKS BELOW.

"HUGGER MUGGER" ... THAT'S MY NAME!

MY NAME MEANS 'SECRET' ...
       MY NAME'S MY GAME!

WHAT I'VE SEEN AND HEARD ...
       JUST BY WATCHING FOLKS BELOW

DON'T THEY REALIZE
       WHAT THEY SOW
THEY WILL ONE DAY ...
       GET PAID BACK TEN-FOLD!

I'M NO ANGEL ...
       I GOT NO WINGS
I DON'T DO MAGIC ...
       GRANTING WISHES ... AIN'T MY THING!

WHAT I DO ... DO
       IS LOOK AND LISTEN ...
WATCHING ALL THE FOLKS BELOW.

WHAT I SEE ...
       IS SO MUCH BETTER ...
THEN WATCHING ANY TV SHOW!

(THIS IS ONE OF FIVE (5) SONGS IN THE SHOW!)

WHAT IS A PRISON?

*It was several years ago that I developed some cartoon characters that I called 'Angel Imps'. Then I put them all in a story in which I included well-known, famous quotes. The small booklet was intended for a very small audience ... my grandchildren. (I dedicated the booklet to both my son, Ashley and my oldest grandson, Stephen ... both took their own lives at the age of 17.) One of the Chapters . . . **"What is a Prison?"** . . . is appropriate for inclusion in this book.*

WE'RE NO ANGELS ... WE'RE IMPS!

Twinkle noticed that Angel Angus had stopped the cloud directly over a statue of a man in front of a building in the middle of the city. "Why are you stopping here?" inquired the young Imp.

"You see that statue, Twinkle? It's there to commemorate a man who helped bring about 'prison reform'. His name was Thomas Mott Osborne."

Pointing eastward, Angel Angus tells Twinkle, "it's over there that we're going next ... into that large walled-in facility ... it's a prison and it's where Mr. Osborne began his life's work."

Twinkle's voice quivered as he spoke, "Wow! That's got to be one scary place!"

When the cloud was directly over the prison, Angel Angus lowered it to the roof of the administrative building and then said, "Today your training will include a closer look at what's going on inside the walls of this place."

"But what exactly is a prison?" Twinkle asks.

"It's where crying and laughter are not allowed," responded Angel Angus. They enter the building and travel along a corridor until they come to a tier.

WHERE
CRYING   NOR   LAUGHTER
    is   ALLOWED   ...

Twinkle noticed that everything was gray ... the buildings had been built with stones of gray and even the yard was an endless slab of gray concrete. From their vantage point, Twinkle could find no evidence of anything green growing.

It was early morning. Some of the inmates were already dressed and waiting for their cell doors to open.

Twinkle could not help but notice that many of the men were in good physical shape ... some were doing stretching exercises, while others were doing push-ups and sit-ups.

Aware of what Twinkle was thinking, Angus responded, "It's important that they take good care of themselves."

Twinkle snapped with a comeback, "They would have to because they belong to the state, right?"

They moved along the corridors, observing all that was going on inside, Angus pointing out many injustices which were being imposed on the inmates by some of the guards. "Ralph Waldo Emerson was right when he said,

"The money in courts and prisons is very ill laid out and their distrust of one another is expensive. We're seeing the truth of this statement today," he told Twinkle.

It became clear to Twinkle that some – in positions of authority – were overlooking what the guards were doing.

They arrived at a remote area at the prison's center ... at a place called: 'The Hole'. It was evident that the inmate in chains had already been subjected to a beating.

"Why do they torture him?" Twinkle asked.

Angus was quick to respond, "No doubt because they have discovered his wants or his desires."

He motioned to Twinkle to move on to the next room where the electric chair was housed. "The recent decision by the U.S. Supreme Court to support the death penalty affirms that Americans are relinquishing their last hope to hold to the Christian heritage. I say this because the teachings of Christ included 'forgiveness' and the Court's decision to uphold this is diametrically opposite to forgiveness. Jesus said, "there is one commandment which is far greater than all the rest ... to do unto others as you would have them do unto you ... that you love your enemies ... and when they would harm you, then help them!" He even encouraged those who believed in Him ... 'to go into the prisons and help the prisoners'. Christ even said, "to forgive murderers'."

Twinkle looked at the electric chair for a very long time. "This was probably the most difficult lesson that mankind might ever be faced with," he thought.

After a long silence, sensing Twinkle's dilemma, Angus asked, "What would you like to say?"

A sigh preceded a long pause ... Twinkle spoke softly and slowly, "What I was taught to believe is that Christ tried to impart to his followers that 'it would be far better if man was taught their duty rather than use death as a reward'."

Angel Angus responded, "When the BOSS ended all of the Commandments with a period, He didn't intend man to replace it with a comma and interpret it whatever way man wanted to!"

Twinkle was quick with an answer, "You're referring to the one that says: 'THOU SHALL NOT KILL.', right?" Then the young Imp added, "And that electric chair there ... it really contradicts that Commandment, doesn't it?"

"Yep!" the elder imp replied. "But it also contradicts the 'teachings' of Christ."

Angel Angus continued, "Even Saint Augustine – a man who was guilty of many misdeeds – said, 'It does not please good people when an evil man, even a heretic, is put to death'. Be aware Twinkle, many of the insights of the Saints stemmed from their experiences as a sinner first. Every saint had a past and every sinner has a future."

Angus continues, saying, "Unfortunately, Christ's teachings of 'forgiveness' still upsets some folks ... even those who call themselves 'Christians' ... who choose to stay blind to what He said. Christ understood that as long as 'an eye for an eye' was the way judgment was to be meted out, there would be a continuum of man's injustice to man."

After a brief pause, he continued, "He came to prove that He could do what He said 'all people must do' and that was to forgive. He set Himself up as an 'example'. As He was nailed to the cross, He proved by His own words that He was able to forgive those who had crucified Him by saying, "forgive them Father ... for they know not what they do'."

"He also said, 'to not judge'," Twinkled added. "When men judge, they are like other men," Angus responded, "but when they forgive, then they are like Him."

But" why does GOD love them?" inquired the young Imp. (The youngster seated himself, cross-legged ... prepared to hear a longer discourse because of his question.)

Angus was eager to respond, "Anders Nygren said it best when he said, 'When it is said that GOD loves man, this is not a judgment on what man is like, but on what GOD is like.' Even George Bernard Shaw said, 'assassination on the scaffold is the worst form of assassination because there it is invested with the approval of society'. Others have opposed capital punishment. There's Charles Dickens who wrote in a letter dated 3/16/1846 to the Daily News: 'Though every other man who wields a pen should turn himself into a commentator on the scriptures ... not all their united efforts, pursued through our united lives, could ever persuade me that executions are Christian'. Dostoevsky believed that 'murder by legal sentence is worse than murder because to kill for murder is a punishment incomparably worse than the crime itself'. What is unfortunate is that the ears of many Christians have become deaf to words once expressed by these important men, as well as many others ... including the words of Jesus and Guatama the Buddha."

"Why don't the clergy discuss the topic of Capital Punishment from their pulpits?" Twinkle asked.

Angus replied, "No doubt they fear losing members from their congregations and that would, of course,mean

less money in the collection plates ... for them."
"Here's another question for you ... why is their a
blindfold on Lady Justice?" Twinkle asked.
"Perhaps she's blindfolded because she might not like
some of the things done in her name if she could see them,"
Angus replied.
"Then life on earth for humans is really about the
opportunity for them to go through all sorts of injustices ...
which can also be called 'tests' ... which will then require
them to forgive others who put them through it ... is that
correct?" Twinkle inquired of his teacher.

"Yep! And even when it hurts A LOT! It's a series
of 'tests' they must pass," replied Angus. "They must be
prepared at all times to put on their work clothes."

Twinkle was quick to respond, "Then life on earth is really a proving ground ... an opportunity to grow ... and folks need to have their work clothes ready at all times!"

"Indeed they must!" Angus replied.

Twinkle paused, then continued, "I'm thinking about what you said about Lady Justice and why she might be blindfolded. I'm thinking the reason why she's got the blindfold on is because people should stand out of her way ... especially if she's blindfolded like that!"

They reached the outside gate and paused. Angus looked back and spoke once more, "It isn't just criminals who take the law into their own hands, judges often do it too. There are too many judges who believe in law and order, as long as they can lay down the law and give the orders. Those in positions of authority too often display an overconfident dogmatic assumption that they are in a position to know all there is to know about GOD. And it's because of this that America is in the chaotic state it is today. Clearly the nation has become a land where lawns are well-kept ... and laws are not!"

"Today's lesson was about forgiveness and I really do understand the whole concept of it a lot better," Twinkle told Angus. "It must be very painful ... and truly, a most difficult thing for people to be able to do. It really is the hardest test of all, right?"

Angus replied to Twinkle, "Indeed, it is so! And if they ask GOD for forgiveness, they will be forgiven; however, if they ask their fellowman, well ... they might be scorned, probably condemned, even laughed at ... but rarely forgiven!"

Angel Angus was quick to respond, "You are INDEED correct! What Mark Twain said about ACTIONS, he said it best, 'the difference between the right action and the almost right action is the difference between the lightning and the lightning bug'." *Both chuckled as they walked over to the cloud and stepped on.* *They were soon directly over the Court House ... only three blocks from the prison.*

The young novice became engrossed in what was going on inside a courtroom, directly beneath the cloud they were floating on. *"There's something I don't understand about humans and that is ... what is it that keeps their courts functioning?"*

"It's plain and simple, Twinkle," responded the elder spirit, "it's their ignorance of the law."

Twinkle was quick with his comeback, "But the way I see it is that in most cases, the law protects only those who can afford to hire a good lawyer!"

The older spirit knew his young charge was correct and he acknowledged him by saying, "Twinkle, you are absolutely correct." Without pausing he continued, "And what is also unfortunate is that the laws are written in a language which is too difficult for the average person to understand. If laws were rewritten in simple language so that everybody could understand their meaning, a great number of attorneys would have to go to work for a living."

The young spirit smiled at his guru's reply and he retorted with his own observations. "And so lawyers write words that make no sense ... so that judges who have to use common sense ... can decide which lawyers make the most sense!" And then he paused ... adding, "Is that it?"

"Yep! You got it Twinkle!" the elder replied. "And," he replied, "don't forget the fact that ignorance of the law is exactly what keeps their higher courts functioning."

"And what about those who go against the grain of God's laws?" Twinkle asked.

"Well they shouldn't complain if they get splinters!"

Angel Angus responded, as he moved to the highest pinnacle on the cloud they were riding, continuing to speak as he stepped upward. "Man is an able creature. He has made 32,647,389 laws and hasn't yet improved on the Ten Commandments." Seating himself in a lotus position, he continued, "Moses was one of the greatest law givers because he was satisfied to keep the Ten Commandments short and to the point ... and that shows clearly that he was not an ordinary lawyer."

The young spirit was quick to respond, "How fortunate that Moses didn't have to submit the Ten Commandments to a staff of lawyers for approval!" The two Imps chuckled. Angel Angus continued, "I like what George Bernard Shaw said about today's modern court ...that "if Jesus had been indicted in a modern court, he would have been examined by two psychiatrists; found to be obsessed by a delusion; declared to be incapable of pleading; and sent to an asylum'."

Because the tone of their conversation was beginning to bog down, Angel Angus decided he'd share a joke with his young charge. "Did you hear what happened at the Pearly Gates yesterday?"

Immediately Twinkle's eyes lite up ... he loved to hear the gossip at the gate. "What happened? Tell me, tell me!!"

"An attorney arrived and the welcoming committee was a bigger group than usual. He was impressed because Moses was there, also the Buddha, Mohammed, Saint Peter and, of course, Jesus. A few Saints showed up also. Well, you can imagine the attorney was overwhelmed by the turnout and asked Saint Peter, 'Does everyone get this kind of welcome upon arriving here?' St. Peter responded, 'No, but this is a special occasion because it isn't very often we can welcome an attorney of such an advanced age.' The

attorney was quick to respond, "What advanced age? I'm only 43 years of age." St. Peter was quick to reply, "Well, not according to the hours you billed'."

Angel Angus noticed that Twinkle was smiling, realizing that the young Imp had gotten the meaning of the joke he'd told him. He then added, "Remember Twinkle, that a test of good religion is whether you can make a joke of it."

It was time to go. They hovered across the yard, stepped onto their cloud and drifted upward and off toward the sunset.

+ + + + + + + + + +

THE HEALERS – MY TEACHERS

It was Dr. Elisabeth Kubler-Ross who said that *"over the the centuries, death has drawn great scrutiny and a distinct turning away. Most preferred to shut the darkness out by keeping the door slammed on death."* But all that changed in 1969 when this world-renowned psychiatrist wrote her landmark book, *"On Death and Dying"*... a book that marked the beginning of the end of the age of denial about what happens to us as we die. The passage which follows is taken from her book:

"At the moment of transition, you're never, ever alone. You're never alone now, but you don't know it. But at the time of transition, your guides, your guardian angels, people whom you have loved and who have passed on before you, will be there to help you in this transition. We have verified this beyond any shadow of doubt, and I say this as a scientist. Most of the time it is a mother or father, a grandparent, or a child ... if you have lost a child. It is sometimes people that you didn't even know were 'on the other side' already."

When astronaut Dr. Edgar Mitchell founded the Institute of Noetic Sciences (INS) in 1971, the investigation of *'mediumship'* became one of the areas of focus for the institute. A core group of their scientists and researchers eventually published a book on the subject and a new name was given to it – CHANNELING – which is also the name of their book. Thus the *'stamp of approval'* was given to it and *'communication with the other side'* was recognized as possible!

Teachers Who Were Healers

Lila Piper, PhD. *(Sociology)*

The late Dr. Lila Piper was a well-known grapho-analysist who accompanied me into the prison where she conducted a three (3) hour workshop for twenty-five (25) inmates.

Dr. Piper was the wife of the late Dr. Raymond Piper, Philosophy Department Chairman at Syracuse University. They'd met in India during the early 30's and witnessed several paranormal events. Their book on *"Cosmic Art"* was ahead of its' time. In the book there are photos of their impressive art collection from around the world.

When this woman -- in her early 80's at the time -- was told by the prison guard that she'd have to walk through the yard, among hundreds of inmates, she responded, "I'd expect they'd know I was there for a good reason."

She impressed the large gathering of prisoners who were told – *only favorable things were said about them ...* simply by her looking at their handwriting.

Later, as a guest in my home, she impressed several invited local professional people who were aware of who she was and wanted to meet her. "For years," she told them she'd "been a consultant to several major companies, evaluating the hand writing of their top applicants." She'd also been called as an 'expert witness' in two well-known court cases, "to attest to whether the signatures on the documents in question were, in fact, signatures of the decedents."

The importance of handwriting was impressed on all who heard Dr. Piper speak that evening. Her remarkable demonstration of interpreting someone's handwriting was convincing to even the admitted "doubtful psychiatrist" who acknowledged her ability. The several professional individuals who came to my home to meet her that October evening openly admitted that "the proof of its credibility was proven to one and all!"

Dr. Piper says that "handwriting is not only a way of knowing a great deal about someone's personality but it is even a more valuable 'tool' in helping young children overcome their 'insecurities'."

Dr. Peter Guy Manners – *(Mentioned in an earlier chapter, it was Dr. Manners who I'd first met in Auburn, N.Y. in 1975 and then later on a trip to England in 1981, where I visited him at his clinic and he acknowledged my "having had a 'past life experience' two days earlier." He also acknowledged his own belief in 'past lives' ...having known (me) in a previous lifetime ... "when we were together in Spain.")*

Dr. Manners studied and collaborated with many outstanding scientists, including Dr. Hans Jenny *(Switzerland)* and Dr. Harold Saxon Burr of Yale University *(U.S.)*.

He researched the use of Cymatics and biomagnetics for medical diagnosis and treatment, including the healing effects of certain sound vibrations and harmonics on the structure and chemistry of the human body, as well as the importance of sound and light in our natural environment.

Dr. Manners was awarded the _Dag Hammarskjold Merit_ _of Excellence_ for _'benefits to humanity';_ the Academe _Diplomatique (De La Paix)_; and the _Diploma of Honour_ in bio-energetic medicine (Moscow) for his contribution to research and development of bio-magnetic medicine.

Without a doubt, my friendship with this most remarkable man had a profound effect on my life. I feel so blessed for having witnessed what 'sound frequencies' can do!

(It was the work of an early 18th century German physicist Ernst Chladni – the 'father of acoustics' – that the idea of vibration could be demonstrated by laying thin layers of sand on a thin metal plate and then set them vibrating; thus observing the patterns that were made in response to different sound stimuli.)

Dr. Manner continued the work of Dr. Hans Jenny, a Swiss doctor, artist, and researcher whose book: _"Cymatics –_ _The Structure and Dynamics of Waves and Vibrations"_ wasn't published until 1967. In this book, published in both German and English, it showed what happens when one takes various materials like sand, water, or iron filings, and places them on vibrating metal surfaces. _(When this is done, shapes and motion-patterns appear. Some of these patterns are nearly perfectly ordered and are stationary. Others develop in a turbulent, organic fashion, and are constantly in motion.)_

Dr. Jenny used crystal oscillators and used them in his invention of what he called a _tonoscope_ ... using them to vibrate plates and membranes.

One of the most fascinating discoveries he made was that

the vowels of Hebrew and Sanskrit, when toned into his media, formed the actual patterns of the letters themselves! Unfortunately modern languages did not have this same effect. *(All of which leads to the speculation that there may be some truth in the concept of a "sacred language" — an actual, physical reason why the recitation of sacred mantras and texts may have real healing properties.)*

Dr. Jenny thought that evolution was a result of *vibrations.* He believed that "the vibrations of one level of organization – such as the level of cells ... each one being unique would combine themselves to create glands and organs and so on, each new level being a harmonic of the previous one." Jenny saw that we "could heal the body with *sound* by under-standing how different frequencies influence the genes, cells, and organs of the body." Out of his early work in the 1920s – as well as that of other scientists in the decades that followed – came the reality of using sound to transmute diseased cells into their healthy counterparts.

Enter the Age of Miracles

It was Sir Peter Guy Manners who collated the work that had been done in previous cymatics research from which he developed from it ... the *Therapy of Cymatics.*

Stated more simply: "*Cymatics therapy uses a toning device to transmit into diseased areas of the body, the signature of healthy organs and tissues.*"

As part of his early training, he and his fellow students would observe doctors in the process of treating their patients. A patient would come in with a complaint of a headache and the doctor would say, "Take these two tablets." The patient leaves but then comes back in a fortnight or so and says, "Those tablets did the trick, but now I've got a little tummy upset." Students would witness the doctor give the patient some different tablets and it would happen again, the same patient returns and says, "'Oh, those tablets were wonderful, but now I've got diarrhea, you see." *(The students realized, "what started with one patient ... is now three patients!")*

Knowing that there had to be a better way of healing than what was being taught in medical school, Dr. Manners decided to do some traveling around the world to find out what other *options* were being used for treating patients. He spent more time in Germany because he liked the research they were doing there. He studied in both Russia and later, the United States.

Somewhere in his travels, Dr. Manners met up with Dr. Hans Jenny. "He was interested in making forms and shapes with sound, and these coincided with the forms and shapes of anatomy and physiology." This observation resulted in a renewal interest in Cymatics – aka: Bio-Resonance ... *a therapy which uses sound to transform diseased tissue into its' healthy counterpart.*

Cymatics probes are used to transmit bio-resonance energy, in the form of electronic pulses, from the Cymatics instrument directly to human tissue. Another method of application is through fluids and/or sound. Water or a homeopathic preparation is placed on a Bio-resonance Energizer, which imprints the bio-energetic patters into the solution. Also, there are units which can transmit bio-energy patterns into a hydrotherapy unit. Yet another unit combines bio-energetic frequencies with color. *(It was my belief that "the sound of the frequency could have the same desired effect on cell" ... and Dr. Manners agreed.)*

Dr. Manners believed he'd proved that "there no difference between the energetic pattern of an object and the object itself, since we are made of energy. Therefore, if we transmit a healthy frequency into the diseased tissue, we cause it to identify itself and thus, take on the 'correct frequency' and the result is a restored and/or return to healthy tissue."

When asked what brings people to Cymatics therapy, Dr. Manners said, "They choose it because most want to move out of the drug scene." *(He often stressed that!)*

At least in the U.K., Cymatics has earned scientific recognition because as a scientist, Dr. Manners developed the techniques that could be explained and quantified, and when the results were proven predictable, he knew what would happen ... he was able to transmit a certain combination of frequencies into the tissue and correct it!

The instrument that is used to transmit sound vibrations into the human body is currently known as the Mark VI. *(It has replaced Mark I through V.)* "This instrument," Dr. Manners says, "holds up to 390 commutations of frequencies, sounds which will regenerate organs and tissues in the body."

Cymatics and The Fountain of Youth

Perhaps the most exciting possible application of Cymatics is that it has the potential to reverse the aging process.

"When you're born," Dr. Manners said, "every cell multiplies. Then, at puberty, the frequency patterns of the cells change, and instead of multiplying, cell replaces cell. As we age, cells still replace each other, but the tempo slows down."

Dr. Manners is convinced that "it's only a matter of time when we will be able to prevent the slowing down of cell replacement and this will be done with sound. If we take a frequency sample of your DNA at age 18, and save it, then later, if we transmit this frequency to your cells, they will rejuvenate."

Although Sir Peter Guy Manners is an 'M.D.', he no longer administers drugs because he says, "drugs are destructive." He calls the type of medicine he practices as *constructive.* And, although in the United States *constructive* healing modalities go under the name of 'alternative therapy', in the United Kingdom they are referred to as <u>Advanced Medicine</u>. Although the doctors who practice it are constantly being hounded by professional and governmental organizations, in his case it got him 'knighted' … thus the title of: Sir!

"It used to be, when doctors didn't know how to heal an arm or a leg, they just amputated it," Manners said. "By the year 2010, medicine – as it's known today – will be as out of date as chopping off limbs. And so, prepare to accept the wonders of technology as established, scientific fact. Miracles will become the natural thing." *(He said this in 1985.)*

"Miracles," concludes Dr. Manners, "were simply things people didn't understand. Today, we can explain miracles. Miracles fit right in with advanced technology."

A comprehensive explanation of 'Vibrational Therapy' *(aka: Cymatics)* can be found on the following http website: www.soundhealersassociation.org/dr-peter-guy-manners-vibrational-thereapy. The website: cymatics.org.uk. provides even more information.

<u>Dr. Michael Glass</u> was a psychiatrist who had his practice in Ithaca, New York for several years. *(I'd heard through a friend that he only practiced 'homeopathic medicine' and so*

I phoned him and confirmed that.) When I told him I was "reaching out to people in the health care field who were practicing medicine in an 'unconventional' way" and I also asked, "if there would be any interest in being a participant in a series on 'wellness' at the local community college?" *(He was told that the pay would only be a very small stipend of $50.)* He surprised me with an immediate response by saying he "would be happy to participate in the series."

Over a period of several years he continued to participate in other local workshops with me, as well as talking before other groups. *(Both in 1994 and 1995, the workshop series he participated in was offered at both Cayuga Community Colleges in Auburn and Fulton, New York.)*

The thing that surprised me most about him was the fact that he no longer prescribed prescription drugs to his patients … they were only treated with homeopathic cell salts! As most are aware, history tells us that "homeopathic medicine originated in Ancient Greece." However, according to Dr. Glass "it is the medicine of the future!"

 A good website where one can get a comprehensive understanding of 'homeopathic' is by going to: *http://www.1-800homeopathy.com/what-is-homeopathy/*

Using homeopathy remedies in my own practice proved – *time and time again* – to work!

One story I have often shared involves a close friend who phoned me to tell me her neighbor "has been given a prescription that would cost nearly $300. to treat her shingles." My response was "take her to the health store in *town and you'll get the homeopathic remedy for shingles for under $10." And she did take it ...and it worked!*

After Dr. Glass's wife passed away, he joined up with his son – their only child – who has a homeopathic practice in England.

Dr. Deborah Malka, MD, PhD

I first met Dr. Malka MD, PhD at <u>Land of Medicine Buddha</u> where she was conducting a *series* of workshops related to *'energy medicine'*.

Her easy-to-follow instructions surprised everyone. *(Simply by holding one's hand six inches above the body, one could sense changes that were emanating from the body, as we moved our hand over it.)* We were surprised to also discover that at those places where we sensed any 'change' that the individual told us they had experienced a previous injury there. We also were able to locate existing problems with a few people who were currently dealing with them.

Dr. Malka is one of the small number of doctors in the State of California that offers medical marijuana evaluations to provide patients with the ability to use marijuana as a part of their medical treatment under California Proposition 215, also known as the California Compassionate Use Act of 1996. *(Her practice is located in Aptos, Ca.)*

Typically, during an office visit, she will gather information about your medical history and lifestyle in order to evaluate you for treatment options that work for your unique conditions.

Later she became my primary care doctor and I found her to be compassionate, well-trained, and always available by phone.

One major condition she satisfactorily treated me for involved a large lump in my left breast. She prescribed a homeopathic remedy and directed me to also apply a poultice – composed of three (3) herbs – "to be applied over the affected area for a period of seven (7) days" I did as I was told and at the end of day ten, it was gone!

A 'hair analysis' is a first-step when becoming Dr. Malka's patient. "Without knowing if there are any mineral deficiencies, we're ignoring what may prove helpful to becoming well," she told me. *(The opposite can also apply ... sometimes we can have too much of an element!)*

(New York is the only state in the U.S. that does not allow a person to have a 'hair analysis' done by a medical doctor. There is one exception ... it's done to 'confirm' drugs in the system!)

Certainly it makes sense that if there's a deficiency of say – *potassium* – then the taking of it would certainly 'correct' the problem! *(As a naturopathy doctor, I'm aware that it is the deficiencies of minerals that often are the cause of most health problems!)*

Dr. Clif Sanderson
Dr. Sanderson was born in New Zealand (Aotearoa) in 1939. He succumbed in 2013. He became known internationally as a creative thinker, mystic and inspirational teacher. He made his first attempt to merge science, mysticism and

spirituality while researching and directing the documentary
"God Doesn't Play Dice" in 1986 for Australian Television.
His curiosity and passion turned him into a non-stop traveler,
explorer and student of different healing traditions around
the world.

The effectiveness of his ground breaking approach – *Deep*
Field Relaxation™ – has been thoroughly researched by
German and Russian scientists.

Long before quantum physics theory became commonly
known, he started applying consciousness and intention for
purposes of healing and transformation. Whenever others tell
of the impossible, Clif has invariably broken through that
belief with innovative, original and inspirational tools.

Dr. Sanderson tested his own beliefs in the "real field" by
accepting an invitation to do volunteer work with the victims
of the Chernobyl disaster in Belarus and Russia in 1990.
(He volunteered his efforts!) He also participated in
numerous medical research projects into the effects of
energy medicine and intention in treating radiation related
illnesses. The Russian Ministry of Health acknowledged
Clif's contribution with the special "Award for Humanitarian
Service to Medical Science".

*(The author met him at Land of Medicine Buddha where he
conducted a series of workshops that covered topics related
to his work. I was also privileged to have had a private two-
hour conversation with him about his personal beliefs,
related to death and dying.)*

Dr. Lavona Stillman

Dr. Stillman had the first hypnotherapy college in California.

I attended her classes over a period of three (3) years and was awarded my diploma as a *Hypnotherapist* in 1994. *(I was one of the fortunate few who also had the opportunity to work in her clinic for an entire year.)*

While I lived in California during the 1990s, she and I served together on the board of directors of the Universal Church of the Master, based in San Jose. *(She later became the President of UCM and I was fortunate to be one of her closest friends.)*

Hypnotherapy is – *without a doubt* – one of the most effective *'tools'* in helping others! *(Rather than have to deal with numerous therapy sessions, all can be accomplished in a handful of hypnotherapy visits.)*

Personally I believe that 'self-hypnosis' should be taught to high school students … for a variety of reasons that include being able to control bleeding!

The results of its' success is beyond what can be imagined possible … but it really is possible!

Lobo Wolf

I attended Lobo Wolf's basic dowsing class in November 1977 … along with twenty-five others … mostly retired mining engineers, geologists, etc. We were there to learn how to *dowse for water, oil, locating treasure, finding caves, etc. … but for me it was being able to locate lost and missing people.*

Certainly the origin of 'dowsing' is lost in antiquity.

The advantages of learning dowsing has *(for me)* been many times rewarded … and I'm excluding 'monetarily'! (Even helping to find sources of water for folks can be a BIG plus! I was surprised to discover that 5th graders can *(usually)* find it quite easily … which I've often witnessed – in part – because I've taught them how to do it in an outdoor classroom setting. *(I shared one story in Chapter V.)*

Over the years many have experienced what is possible. I've been fortunate to have been able to find *'ley lines'* by *dowsing* … which Native Americans have known how to do since the beginning of their time on the North American continent.

Although Lobo Wolf has since passed away, the organization he founded is still up-and-running and his http/website can be found at: www.treasurenet.com/forums/dowsing/375544.

It is the American Society of Dowsers that is probably the most well recognized group that is known to the American public. They organized in 1960 and for years the ASD would meet in Danville, Vermont in September to hear lectures on the latest state of their art. However, because their numbers have increased into the hundreds, they have to meet in other places around the United States where they can be accommodated. Their members include the most skilled dowsers – ranging from water dowsers to seekers of minerals and lost objects, energetic dowsers, esoteric dowsers – and a great deal more. Check out their http website: dowsers.org/

+ + + + + + + + + + +

182

A BELIEF IN SPIRIT POSSESSION

A BELIEF IN EXORCISM

This writer is well aware of what's been happening over the last few decades, as it relates to the alarming number of Americans embracing *mysticism* by democratizing it, diversifying it and taking it mass market. How unfortunate that this occurred!

It is important to note that in 2004, worried about the rise of the occult, Pope John Paul II asked Cardinal Ratzinger, the head of the Vatican's Congregation for the Doctrine of the Faith – who went on to become Pope Benedict XVI – "to direct bishops around the world to appoint and train more exorcists in the dioceses."

On the topic of "exorcism" the Wikipedia website states: "Spirit possession is a term for the belief that animals, extraterrestrials, gods, or spirits can take control of a human body. The concept of spirit possession exists in many religions, including *Christianity, Buddhism, Wicca, Hinduism, Island* and *Southeast Asian* and *African* traditions."

In a 1969 study funded by the National Institute of Mental Health, "spirit possession beliefs were found to exist in 74% of a sample of 488 societies in all parts of the world. Depending on the cultural context in which it is found, possession may be considered voluntary or involuntary and may be considered to have beneficial or detrimental effects to host. Within possession cults, the belief that one is possessed by spirits is more common among women than men."

Although Islam is not mentioned in the above paragraph as a religious group that believes in *"spirit possession"*... there is one verse in the Qur'an that says that *"those who act as if they were possessed or controlled by a satanic touch should seek refuge in Allah from the accursed devil"* and in another verse, *"the devil has no power of influence over those whom God has guided."*

In Augustin Calmet's *"Treatise on the Apparitions of the Spirits and on Vampires or Renants"* ... he writes that *"the Egyptians believed that when the soul of a man who has died a violent death, it remains near the body and nothing can make it go away; it is retained there by sympathy; several have been seen sighing near their bodies which were interred."* *(The individual is "earth bound".)*

Many other ancient civilizations, such as those in China, Babylon and Greece believed that the only way to exorcise *bad spirits* from anyone who possessed a *bad spirit* was to subject the person to a ritualized ceremony that frequently involved direct physical attacks on the sufferer's body in an attempt to force out the demons *(e.g. through torture, flogging or starvation).*

One only has to go back to the mid-1500s when the *Spanish Inquisition* occurred and the Church subjected hundreds of thousands of people to torture and even death because it was believed that the people were 'under the spell of evil' if they were not practicing Catholics.

Even today in most Christian Churches the clergy continue to preach against those who foretell the future. They believe that those who foretell the future and perform prophesies "receive their power from an evil spirit and – whether good or evil – in the end they never lead anyone to what is truly good." *(However, in the Bible – Book of Corinthians – Chapter 14; vs. 1-12, it says "there will be those who can see spirit and can perform prophesies"* ... but there is no mention in any of the Bible verses that state the person is *evil!* Instead, the Bible says those who can ... have <u>*gifts*</u>!)

A PSYCHIATRIC DISEASE?

On the Wikipedia website it says that *"spirit possession is now recognized as a psychiatric or medical diagnosis by the DSM-IV or the ICD-10."* Listed are mental conditions that the untrained person/novice may believe are people who are really possessed ... "those with a psychosis, hysteria, mania,Tourette's syndrome, epilepsy, schizophrenia, or dissociative identity disorder including involuntary, uncensored behavior, and an extra-human, extra-social aspect to the individual's actions."

In a *Psychology Today* article (12/31/13) by Psychologist Graham C. L. Davey – <u>Spirit Possession and Mental Health</u> – he writes about *"the many cultures that still believe that unusual behavior is caused by spirit possession."* He says that *"spirit possession is simply used to try and explain the effects of psychopathology-related experiences, but are also regularly used by many cultures to control and coerce individuals to do acts of extreme brutality."*

Davey stresses the need for help *"of many who have been suffering debilitating and distressing psychological problems who still are being persecuted and physically abused rather than offered the support and treatment they need."*

Demonic possession is talked about in the Bible. *"Christ cast seven demons out of Mary Magdalene." (Mark 16 v. 9) "He also cast demons into the swine and they ran off the cliff to their death." (Matt. 8 v. 32).*

Sermons in churches today – on the topic of *Demonic Possession* – are rarely given and the reason, according to the clergy "is because the attendance in church would soon diminish!"

Many earth-bound spirits stay because of their addictions while on earth … *to alcohol, drugs, etc.* The *spirits* will typically attach themselves to a living person who is also addicted … so they can continue to *'get their fix'!* Thus those living with addictions often allow themselves to become *possessed. Possession* is possible for other reasons as well. A mentally ill person may become the vehicle for a deceased mentally ill person who wishes to stay attached to another mentally ill person.

What is perhaps the most disturbing type of *possession* can occur when someone under the influence of alcohol or drugs, or in a state of depression or anger, becomes the host for the entry of a *demonic* type of entity. *(This is what has happened to the person who becomes a serial killer and, as a result, the 'possessed individual' has no control over their own actions! If 'put to death in the chair' the entity goes to another person … and possesses them!)*

(Let me again emphasize that 'demonic possession' has a wide range of possibilities. For example, coming up in another chapter of this book is what occurred the night that one of my children was doing drugs and displayed a total disregard for the dead by being disrespectful in the cemetery

when 15 years old. To this day, I am convinced my child became demonically possessed that night. Many of the actions throughout my child's lifetime bear witness to it!)

According to the **Bible** – we have *'free will'!* But Christ warns that we will be judged not only by our actions but our thoughts as well! And, although we may be able to restrain outward behavior, it's our thoughts that can have some of the more serious consequences. Therefore, thoughts must also be correct! Since both *correct* and incorrect thoughts can manifest ... it is the thought *'for someone to be harmed'* that can occur! And, it is often the demonically possessed individual who carries out the other person's thought, by performing the misdeed!

Keep in mind that *'a silent prayer'* is done through a quiet thought process … never spoken! A prayer can also be spoken aloud! Therefore, be *(so)* careful what you think … because thoughts can *manifest* ... and they often do! *(Whether positive or negative ... thoughts can manifest!)*

As defined in Webster's dictionary:

Saint: *"a supernatural, incorporeal being, as a ghost ... an angel or demon."*
Angel: *"one of a class of spiritual beings; a celestial attendant of God ... a messenger ... a guardian spirit. A deceased person whose soul is regarded as being in heaven."*
Demon: *"an evil spirit."*

The Catholic Church describes a SAINT as "someone who has been canonized as being extremely holy."

In Buddhism, there is considerable credit given to 'bodhisattvas'. And, as defined by Webster: <u>A bodhisattva is "a person who has attained enlightenment but who postpones Nirvana in order to help others to attain enlightenment</u>."

There are many examples throughout history of these holiest of people. In this lifetime, Mother Theresa was an example of a bodhisattva, as was Pope John Paul. Let me add a bit more proof of this Pope being one!

Mostly it will be only Catholics who will recall that prior to John Paul becoming Pope, there was one who proceeded him who only lived seven days. This occurred in the late fall of 1977. It was on the day John Paul was ordained as Pope that the most remarkable thing happened ... not only in Auburn, but in many other places ... <u>the lilies bloomed</u>!

(A picture of a young boy holding a lily in front of many lilies in bloom, in his grandparents' yard on Owasco Road in Auburn, New York, appeared in the Syracuse Post Standard newspaper on that same day. And, as we all know, they only bloom at Easter time!)

"The fact that the lilies bloomed in this instance," according to Rev. Mae, "is because it is a 'sign' that this Pope will be a good one!" *(And indeed ... that became so!)*

KIRLIAN PHOTOGRAPHY ... as more proof?

Researcher, Dr. Peter Guy Manners (*) shared photos with members of my Parapsychology Group that revealed *a large cloudy mass* attached to the back of mental patients he was visiting in a closed ward. *(Kirlian photography was the process with which those photos were taken.)*

The _Wikipedia_ website says: *"Kirlian photography is a collection of photographic techniques used to capture the phenomenon of electrical coronal discharges. It is named after Semyon Kirlian, who in 1939 accidentally discovered that if an object on a photographic plate is connected to a high-voltage source, an image is produced on the photographic plate. The technique has been variously known as "electrography", "electrophotography", "corona discharge photography" (CDP), "bioelectrography", "Gas Discharge visualization (GDV)","electrophotonic imaging (EPI)",and, in Russian literature, "Kirlianography" ....*

The website further explains the process: *"Photographic film is placed on top of a conducting plate, and another conductor is attached to a hand, a leaf or other plant material. The conductors are energized by a high-frequency high-voltage power source, producing photographic images typically showing a silhouette of the object surrounded by an aura of light."*

(Kirlian photography has been the subject of mainstream scientific research and to a large extent, it has also been used in alternative medicine research.)

It wasn't until 1970, when two Americans, Lynn Schroeder and Sheila Ostrander, published a book, *"Psychic Discoveries Behind the Iron Curtain"* that we first learned of *Kirlian photography* in this country.

Many readers may recall seeing published photographs showing a glow *(aura)* around leaves. *(When my son was in the 7th grade in 1970, he brought home a copy of the Science Weekly Reader and on the front page there was a picture of botanist, Dr. Cleve Baxter whose research confirmed 'plants having emotions' ... this was further enhanced by photos being made public of the leaf's "aura" – ' a glow around the leaves'.)*

In Western religious traditions, you can often see the 'aura' portrayed in art as a *halo* surrounding *saints* or a *deity*. In Eastern religious traditions, it is thought to emanate from the chakras -- or centers of energy within the body and is often depicted as a multicolored body of light surrounding a person. *(Colors match the chakras and endocrine system.)*

For the past few decades Kirlian Photography has been used to reveal important information about a person's emotional energetic state, identifying signs of rising energy-stress, allowing you to address the issue before physical symptoms arise. There are people who are able to "see" *auras* and many who have been trained to know that the colors exhibited in the aura have specific meanings.

For holistic healers, *aura* reading is the art of investigating the human energy field, or the energy fields of other sentient beings. It is a basis for using techniques of holistic healing, and includes such practices as bio energetics, energy medicine, energy spirituality and energy psychology.

In 1995 I met with an *"energy doctor"* who I mentioned in the last chapter. She could not only feel auras but could see them as well. She was able to diagnose my health issues from what she was able to feel outside my body *(aura)*. She ran the diagnostic test to confirm it and she was 100% correct in her diagnosis. Her homeopathy remedies were prescribed that included poultices and a homeopathic remedy.

(My training for my Doctorate in Naturopathy included the study of homeopathy remedies. One of my teachers – Psychiatrist, Dr. Michael Glass – was mentioned also in the previous chapter.)

Christ said we're to "believe in *angels*"... and, according to world renowned psychiatrist, Dr. Elizabeth Kubler-Ross, "they are there." (In her book *"Death and Dying"* she confirms this, "often you're being watched from the *'other side'* by *angels* and sometimes, it's others you have known." *(Perhaps it is the angels who are the ones who are "keeping a list and checking it twice!")*

When it comes to 'reincarnation' ... it really is a matter of living a number of lifetimes ... as many as are needed! Some have already made it to another 'dimension' and the rest of us are still trying to get there. That's why 'choice' (aka: free will) is possible. Not making the right choice(s) is why we come back again and again ... and then one day when we finally wake up, truly committed to making the effort to do what is correct' so that we can 'move on' ... we go to the next 'dimension'!

(I recall telling the inmates I had in my classes that I'd obviously 'blown a number of previous lifetimes' ... because I am back ... and I must continue working at it ... just as they must also!)

+++++++++++++++

WHY I WAIT ... FOR A PRISONER

My involvement with prisoners put me in touch with a select number of gifted inmates who had developed their art skills after coming to prison. The work of one inmate, *James Moore*, in particular stood out. Most of his work was good — and some of it was very good. *(He was also a 'closet' Buddhist.)*

WHO IS HE?

James Moore is convinced that the prison experience offers desperately needed challenges to improve one's condition. He was born with clubbed feet, dislocated hips and underwent twenty-three operations to improve this condition before he was sixteen years old.   He spent most of these years in casts, braces and on crutches. He remembers "only the loneliness, rejection and always the discomfort in his legs," during those times.

When he came to prison he was woefully lacking in coordination – mental and physical – and he had no self-confidence. In order to survive, he had no choice but to change and re-program himself.

James Moore became the fastest and most improved student on the inside. He enrolled in college in Auburn in 1978, earned his A.A. two years later. He went on to earn his B.S. and then his M.A. and M.B.A. By 1991 he had his Ph.D. in Business Management. *(It was from the sale of his paintings that he paid for his education.)* This was a first for anyone on the inside!

He also undertook other challenges to enhance his physical and mental condition: chess, weights, handball and volleyball. He worked in both the plate shop and wood shop in Auburn prison.

Prior to the Attica 'riot' no books were allowed inside that pertained to Eastern philosophy or religions. While he was there he received a book on yoga *(via the underground railroad)*. When he opened the book, "it was as if a bright light had gone on in my head." He said, "I could not put it down. There were so many benefits to reading it — both mental and physical — that helped quiet my monkey mind, to change my philosophy, my whole outlook on myself and the world around me."

He began to meditate in privacy and in secrecy because it was a violation to practice anything other than Christianity. Yoga was considered "sexually promiscuous." Jim's family was Episcopalian, and he was an acolyte until nineteen years of age. The extensive training and the time-and-energy-consuming commitment to it was too limiting. "It did not satisfy my own curiosity," he said. When the time came to choose between a full-time commitment to the church or a job to support himself, he left the church.

It was the book handed to him at Attica, "a bundle of pages, cover less, held together with string, that provided the first missing pieces of the puzzle, answers I had so long sought," he told me. He typed the entire text of the book on onion skin paper so he could pass copies around to others for their benefit.

"Soon we had over fifteen inmates on the gallery attempting to do the exercises and meditations. We had no mats and so cardboard, pieces of blanket, and worn-out clothes were used to sit on. The gallery — normally noisy — was quiet as the men all concentrated and struggled with their practice. We all knew that if we were caught, we would be severely reprimanded. Yet it was very important to us to practice."

"Sitting in meditation requires the right foot on the left thigh, and the left foot on the right thigh, which I was unable to do because of all the surgery done on my feet and legs. And yet, I was born in a lotus position!" He now sits in a dragon position.

The lawsuit which allowed Buddhists to practice was won in 1979. The Senior Chaplain, a Protestant, complained that "he had no money in his current budget with which to help and it would be another year before there would be the monies for the items and supplies the group needed."

It was at that time that Jim approached me for help. Twenty cushions were needed, as well as meditation books and incense. The inmates built the Butsudan, Tamar, and bell stand. A Mohawk Indian friend, a first-rate seamstress, helped me sew the cushions. My church donated monies for books and materials, in exchange for a promised donation of a painting which they would later use as a fund raiser (*Jim provided the painting*).

After contacting the prison chaplain, he agreed to let the items come in to him that following Monday. And the following week, the monks from the Ithaca Zen Center came in and for the first time, sat zazen with the inmates.

That all happened in December of 1980. Jim remembers the first sitting. "The feeling was so wonderful that I was literally floating on air. There was the fragrance of the incense and the sound of the bells which added to my own personal happiness. I knew I was home! The terrible pain in my legs from sitting in an impossible position, unfamiliar to Westerners, did not matter!" Later, when Jim led a three-day retreat, his feet began to bleed. "It did not matter," he said, "I did not feel any pain, I only felt complete solace and peace."

A visitor and friend, Crystal Forestwarren, who makes yearly pilgrimages to India to be with the Dalai Lama, presented them with a white prayer shawl from His Holiness. She draped it over the hand-made wooden altar.

The zendo was also visited by Sasaki Roshi of the Rinzai-Ji sect of Zen, as well as Paul Reps, author of *Zen Bones – Zen Flesh*. Buddhism transcends religion, race, nationality and gender. Jim is convinced that Buddhism can show a Christian how to be a better Christian.

"The sittings are only for those that are willing to truly quiet their monkey minds," Jim points out. "But once the practice is learned, it is then possible to sit in the confinement of one's cell, amid all the noise and confusion, and be free!"

After ten years of regular sittings and retreats, it came time for the monks to leave Ithaca. And so — for most — the inmates continue their practice in their cells, or whenever they walk in the yard.

FIFTY PLUS YEARS OF INCARCERATION

James Moore has been incarcerated for over fifty years. Few have ever done this in one stretch.

"Nearly all the others I knew and started with are either dead, or their whereabouts are unknown," he says. "I ask myself, 'Why am I still here? How have I managed this far when others who seemed more up to the challenge have not?' I know I am a pariah. I know also that Shakyamuni Buddha and the deities have seen to it that what I needed — not what I wanted — but what I needed, was available for me so I could pass all tests and survive karmic attacks. I have to live among men who hate and so I must strive toward not hating in return. The greatest destroyer is the desire to hate. I know that. That is why I am here ... to pass that test!"

In his journal he writes: "I, James Robert Moore, also known by such names as Yo-Toku, Shinto, and more recently as Thubten Tenzin, do hereby write this chronicle as a last scream of self preservation." And of his prison experience, he writes: "Human beings are completely and unavoidably influenced by their surroundings, the unique structure in which they live. The structure of a prison and its population, forces a prisoner to conform his conduct to a certain set pattern."

When asked "if there is spiritual freedom in the surroundings of a prison, even if one is facing a life sentence?" he responded: "My experience has been that man indeed has a choice of action, even in terrible conditions of psychic and physical stress." He quotes Frankel: "Everything can be taken from a person but one thing, the last of the human freedoms, to choose one's attitude in any given set of circumstances, to choose one's own way."

And so Jim writes, "An inmate may retain human dignity even in a prison, bearing sufferings as a genuine inner-achievement. It is this spiritual freedom that cannot be taken away that gives or makes life meaningful and purposeful."

"Most prisoners will agree that the most depressing influence of all is not to know how long one's term of imprisonment will be. A prisoner with a life sentence is unable to aim at an ultimate goal in life. He has no future. Signs of decay set in. Life is uncertain and you are thinking that the worst is yet to come, when in fact it's already over! Most vegetate while a few turn life into an inner triumph.

Nietzche wrote because he understood that 'that which does not kill me, makes me stronger'."

Jim writes, "Sufferings can become achievement and accomplishment. One can derive from guilt the opportunity to change oneself for the better and develop an incentive to act responsibly . . . I did not understand why I should suffer so severely, in so many ways, when I was young. I did not begin to understand until after coming to prison. Without this suffering I would have never experienced growth. I realized this soon after I came into the prison system. I told my service unit counselor that 'I realized I couldn't go any lower unless I died and I had been denied that privilege.' *(The death penalty was abolished in New York State in 1963 which was the year Jim was sentenced.)* "And so," he writes, "since I had not been allowed the pleasure of death, there was only one way, and that was up."

And so, he has done what he needed to do. By going within, he has discovered who he really is. James Moore has never denied his crime. He does not deny the intense pain he caused for others, and the most intense of pain, the hell he created for himself. It is precisely because the inmate has taken responsibility for all of this as his own that he is now changed.

All indications are that he has succeeded in rehabilitating himself within a corrections system that most will agree is not conducive to such human growth. He has become a symbol of hope for many of the inmates, many corrections workers and administrators, and indeed, those who have the ability to truly see who he has become.

"The real miracle is when men who have been treated for many years like beasts persist in retaining their manhood," said Thomas Mott Osborne, State Legislator in May, 1929.

(Mr. Osborne was instrumental in introducing legislation to abolish capital punishment in New York State in the early 1920s.)

THE LAND OF MEDICINE BUDDHA

When this author moved to California in 1989, I learned about Land of Medicine Buddha. I will never forget my reaction to seeing the statue of my patron saint — Saint Francis of Assisi — on the terraced garden in front of where I parked my car, the day I came to Land of Medicine Buddha for the first time.

Signs are indicators of importance and meaning to me and so seeing the statue of Saint Francis was letting me know that I needed to investigate Land of Medicine Buddha. And I soon realized that I had found a place where I would find answers, and so I made a commitment in the Spring of 1993 to volunteer to help there.

Lama Zopa Rinpoche's letter welcoming Jim — "upon his release" — to the Land of Buddha has been a most profound *gift* to both of us. Jim continues to make his practice even stronger and has continued several years of the study of Buddhism. He is also grateful that Lama Zopa Rinpoche sent his book, along with that letter. Jim knows that he's at last found a *teacher.*

The words in the book revealed some of the answers that Jim had been searching for. "I have only deep respect for Lama Zopa Rinpoche," Jim writes, "he provides me with the directions so that I can climb the foothills that surround the mountain that this miserable sack of putrification must surmount."

As for me? My eyes were opened as a result of the prison work experience. It has enabled me to see that some inmates come to love and value life more in prison than when they were free. It is truly amazing — *an almost impossible thing to believe possible* — but it is only through the experience of working with inmates that one is able to perceive the wonderful qualities in some of these people. The Bible says: "There are none so blind as those who refuse to see." *(I now understand what that passage means!)*

The blessing for me that has come is the realization that it is possible to find a diamond in a dung pile. I found one!

+ + + + + + + + + + + + + + + +

ABOUT THE AUTHOR: *Joyce Ann Smith*

Born November 24, 1934, the author grew up in Auburn, New York. She was a twin and the youngest of eight siblings.

Joyce Smith graduated from Central High School in 1952 and was awarded the faculty's highest award for *'Scholarship & Service'.*

Married more than once, she was the mother of five children. She lost one tragically at the age of 17. She is a grandmother of thirteen and great-grandmother of eight.

After her divorce, she returned from California to Auburn in 1971. She went to work as the *Administrative Secretary* to the Superintendent of Auburn Schools. That same year, she and the superintendent co-founded the *Cayuga County Arts Council. (She served as a board member for ten years and as the CCAC's President from 1977 to 1979.)*

She organized a parapsychology group in 1971, composed of several professional people living in the area. They met regularly and in 1974 the group conducted several workshops at the YMCA, donating all the proceeds to the "Y". A workshop series was later offered to inmates in Auburn prison and was well received. The most popular workshop – Astrology – conducted by Dennis Cole, continued for another five years inside the prison.

After Joyce completed her requirements for her broker's license in real estate, she opened her own office in 1973. *(She later completed the requirements for her broker's licenses in both insurance and securities.)*

In 1979, Joyce was offered the position of *Executive Director* of the *Adirondack Regional Arts Council* by the *New York State Council on the Arts*. Prior to her leaving the job in 1983, the LARAC board dedicated the "LARAC 12th Annual Festival" to her *"in recognition of her four years of dedication, timeless work, and commitment to all the Arts in the Adirondack Region."*

In 1983 she was offered the position of *Executive Director* of the *Finger Lakes Arts Council.* She was instrumental in the beginning efforts of restoring the Smith Opera House in Geneva, New York. After leaving the job, the blueprint that she laid down was followed and the restoration work was completed in 1988. *(Violin virtuoso Itzak Perlman spoke about the Smith Opera House on the* Today Show *after having given a benefit performance there, saying "it is acoustically one of the finest houses in existence."* The *"Smith"* was built by *Spiritualist* William Smith in 1892. He later built the first non-denominational college in the nation. Joyce holds a Bachelor's Degree in Business Administration through SUNY's *Empire State College Program.*

In 1989, she returned to California to pursue her doctorate degree in *Naturopathy.* Part of her degree program included a *hands-on* experience in an alternative health clinic in the Santa Cruz area. Areas of concentration included Advanced Hypnotherapy and Cymatics *(sound healing).* Her N.D. degree was awarded in 1995.

While living in California she also completed her ministerial requirements in the field of *healing* and was ordained by the Universal Spiritualist Church of the Master.

(The first step in her religious training began in the 1970's when she completed more than the required 1,500 hours of donated time by working with inmates in Auburn prison.)

+ + + + + + + + + +

Over a period of twenty years her over one-hundred donated *feature articles* appeared in the local Auburn newspaper. Most of her articles highlighted numerous artists and artisans in the area. A wide-variety of other topics published included articles featuring local history. *(Go to the newspaper's website at: AuburnPub.com and in the search engine, enter <u>Joyce Hackett Smith-Moore</u> and an extensive listing of 'feature articles' she's written will appear. Her over one hundred 'letters to the editor' will also appear, showing a wide diversity of her interests.)*

From 2000 to 2015, she donated hundreds of hours to the *Cayuga-Owasco Lakes Historical Society* (COLHS) in Moravia where she served on their board as *Secretary*. She later served two separate terms of two years each as their *President*.

Doing research into her genealogy revealed her direct link to both <u>Presidents Fillmore and Garfield.</u> Her efforts at raising awareness of our *13th U.S. President, Millard Fillmore* – born just outside of Moravia – was acknowledged in a letter by the Town of Summerhill's Historian, Florence Lansdowne who wrote: *"Without your efforts the pavilion that was donated and erected on Fillmore's birth site by the Auburn Steel Company would not have been possible."*

Over the period 2000 to 2010 *(ten years)* her exhibit at the COLHS History House – "<u>*Moravia – The Mecca of Spiritualism*</u>" was a major attraction. The first bus tours to ever visit the museum occurred. *(The exhibit was originally part of a much larger exhibit in 2002 at the Cayuga Museum of History & Art in Auburn, set up by Ellen McHugh, the Director.)*

Over the years, she has donated her services to raising money for a number of non-profit organizations in the area, speaking on the topic of *Spiritualism*.

In 2015 she was honored by the County Legislature as the year's "Senior Citizen of Cayuga County" for her *"thousands of hours of volunteer service."*

+ + + + + + + + + +

A ROSE BY ANY OTHER NAME
by Dr. William T. Stead (*)

To give a little demonstration in a practical way of the diversity of stages to which human life evolves, we may consider as an example a rose bush. Here we have a specimen of life in various stages. There may be, according to the size of the bush, anywhere from twenty to a hundred specimens. In this picture before you, let us imagine that these are human beings instead of roses or buds that are on the bush. We may find two, three or four that have reached perfection. As we examine the bush we find roses in all stages of growth until we actually reach a stage where a tiny bud looks more like a tiny green knot. This is also a member of the family and a brother/sister to the ones who have reached perfection. But, it is utterly impossible for buds which are in their primitive state, even though they belong to the same bush, to sense the consciousness and the life of the fully developed rose. Here we have a complete picture of evolving life as we know it in the human family. The person who has grasped the truth of life does not look down upon his younger brother or younger sister because they happen to be younger than themselves. On the contrary, the person is able through their full conception of life to develop the much needed quality of tolerance, the fruit of knowledge and understanding. We know that our younger brother/sister, who today as yet lacks their own beauty and capacity, will also in time be as fully developed.

(*) <u>Dr. Stead was a Spiritualist and went down with the Titanic in 1912</u>.

A TWIN SISTER – A HALF SISTER!
written by the author

Indeed …
our weight differed greatly!
The first twin weighed eight pounds ...
and the second twin weighed less than three
and the bigger twin … well, that twin was me !

Several decades later …
medical research uncovered
the reasons why there were other differences
the two of us had ... from one another.

For what was discovered
after my mother had gotten pregnant
well … she got pregnant again!
and how that could possibly happen ...
is because a few weeks after getting pregnant
she ovulated again … thus the second twin!

Since this occurred back in 1934
and because research is only now able to tell us
so much about what is possible
there was also something else
that I was surprised to learn!

That even though we were born at the same time
it didn't necessarily make her my 'twin'
for the DNA evidence found
that we were fathered by two different men!

AMEN

The author, Thomas R. Hazard spent eleven (11) days in Moravia, New York and wrote daily accounts of his time spent with the 'medium' Mary Andrews. What follows are 'excerpts' from his book: "Eleven Days At Moravia." What is told here are the actual events that Hazard witnessed. (He went to Moravia as a 'skeptic' and left as a 'believer'!) He later wrote another book: "Mediums and Mediumship."

ELEVEN DAYS AT MORAVIA

DAY ONE: On the 26th of December, 1871, I took an evening train on the New York Central Railroad, at Albany, for Syracuse. Next morning, at six, I took the cars on the same road some twenty-six miles, to the depot at Auburn; thence by omnibus one-half mile, to the depot of the Southern Central Railroad; thence some seventeen miles to Moravia, where carriages were in waiting to take passengers to the far-famed "spirit-house" of Morris Keeler, three-quarters of a mile, for fifty cents each – the whole cost of railroad fare from Boston (via Worcester and Albany), omnibus and back hire included, being less than eleven dollars.

Moravia is a pretty, cozy-looking village of some twelve or fifteen hundred inhabitants, in Cayuga County, State of New York. It is pleasantly situated on the southwesterly declivity and base of a range of hills running along the easterly side of the rich alluvial Owasco valley, which is several miles long and half a mile or more wide. Fortunately, I found a lodging-room vacant at Mr. Keeler's, there being less rush of visitors than usual, owing probably to the domestic festivities of the season. As a general rule, more or less new-comers are necessitated to lodge there.

Though not on the summit, Mr. Keeler's house stands high on the hill. It is nearly new, of two stories, and larger and more commodious and tastily finished than most farm houses. On its western side or end is a light projection or alcove, forming in part the base of a tower or cupola of moderate height, commanding a fine-view of the surrounding country. An apartment of convenient dimensions in the second story, situated beneath this tower, is set apart exclusively for the "spirit-room." Like the rest of the house, this room is neatly finished and very prettily papered, with the exception I shall presently mention. Its furniture, all included, consists of an air-tight stove, a sofa, a kerosene lamp and candlestick, a small paper screen, a piano and some dozen chairs – a large part of which are broken, rickety or disfigured, in consequence of an ill-bred habit in which some are addicted, of tipping back, greatly to the injury of both chairs and carpets."

THE 'SPIRIT CABINET': "A wood cabinet that the *medium* sits inside consists of one common wooden chair and one battered tin trumpet. Except when seances are being actually conducted, the cabinet stands open at all times for inspection."*(It has an aperture (opening) 2' x 3' that is covered with a black cloth.)*

THE MEDIUM: "Mary Andrews is a rather stout, well-formed woman, of medium height, apparently from twenty-five to thirty years of age. She is the mother of three nice little girls, the eldest of whom has been adopted by Mr. and Mrs. Keeler. Mrs. Andrews is comely in face and person, and bright-looking; and if Nature meant to affix the stamp of dishonesty or trickery to her features, it made a transparent mistake. She is very amiable and conversable

with those who approach her with respect and kindness, but
cannot give any explanation of the why and wherefore of the
wonderful phenomena that occur in her presence.

"Shortly after having found employment as a domestic with Mr. and Mrs. Keeler, her extraordinary *medium*
powers were gradually developed with the assistance of Mr.
Keeler.

"There is something undefinable in the atmosphere of
the Keeler house. Everybody under the roof seems cheerful,
happy and contented. I think there may have been some
sixty arrivals whilst I remained, and each and all, with scarce
an exception, seemed to feel at home the moment they
entered the door.

"During the eleven days I stayed, I never left the
house but once, further than the adjoining yard, and then
only for an hour or two. Terribly contrary to my disposition
and usual wont, I always got up in the morning in a cold
room, in January, by candle-light, and lived on the plainest
food; and yet can truly say that I never experienced a
moment's *ennui* or depression of spirit at Moravia."

THE séance: "With the exception of an occasional
private circle, Mrs. Andrews generally holds a *séance* every
forenoon and afternoon, including Sundays, at fifty cents for
each person. If only four or less sit in private, her charge is
two dollars for the whole. The *séance* begins with what is
called a dark circle, the visitors, to the number of eight or
ten, ranging themselves in a semi-circle some eight or ten
feet from the cabinet *(which is not used then)*, on the outside
of the partition of which, directly under the aperture, Mary
sits facing the *circle.* Sometimes the number of visitors
requires the making of two *circles,* one within the other. The
chairs should be arranged in exact order, the feet of all the
sitters kept flat on the floor, and the knees as nearly in a

semi-circle line as practicable. The hands are then joined,
and the light *(a very primitive tallow candle)* is extinguished.
Harmony in the circle is indispensable to secure good
manifestations, and this is greatly promoted by singing, in
which it is better that all or a large portion of the *circle*
should join in. It seems to matter but little what the words
are, provide, they will admit, like "Old John Brown's Body,"
of being pronounced with a vim. This is probably because
they receive closer attention from the members of the *circle,*
and in that way promote harmony by concentrating the
thoughts of all present at one point. Old-fashioned *witches
(probably without knowing why)* used to produce a like
effect by causing their votaries to look steadily at grounds of
tea in a cup. It may be, too, that there is some element that
goes forth from the organs of the singers, that is utilized by
the *spirits,* and made to contribute to the production of *spirit*
voices.

"In these dark *circles,* the phenomena that occur are
quite varied. The floor assumes a tremulous motion, or the
partition of the cabinet is shaken, sometimes violently!
Questions are answered by *spirit-lights* – three appeared as
an affirmative, one and two for negative and doubtful – keys
of the piano are occasionally struck – water is sprinkled in
the faces of the sitters – cold breezes pass around the circle –
stars or lights appear in various parts of the room, and
sometimes engage in playful exhibitions, as if mingling in a
dance. The flapping of something like wings of a large bird
is heard as if close by; and, on two occasions, I and some
others were sprinkled with something that felt cold but not
moist.

"Besides these manifestations, *spirit* voices *(sometimes very distinct)* often join in the singing. The hands and
persons of sitters are patted by *spirit*-friends and generally,

some of these manifest themselves by speaking audibly or in distinct whispers, sometimes at considerable length. Once while I was present, the tin trumpet was thrown out of the opening in the cabinet onto the floor, picked up and spoken through by a *spirit,* then dropped on the floor, and again taken up and thrown back into the cabinet. After some thirty or more minutes have expired, a *spirit*-voice, in a cheerful or jocose tone, *(and generally with a German or Indian accent, though not always)* asks that a light may be struck – and the dark *séance* closes.

"Perhaps this imperfect description may convey to uninitiated readers some idea of the mode that is pursued in obtaining *spirit* manifestations at Moravia, and of the phenomena that occur more or less at every *séance,* so that they can better comprehend what follows, as well as much that has before been published on the subject.

"Men and women who go entirely out of curiosity are very apt to carry with them an adulterated magnetism, which leaves sometimes an odor and a sphere very disagreeable to a more advanced *spirit.*

"Both before and whilst at Moravia, I frequently remarked that I had seen and heard enough to satisfy me beyond doubt of a future state of existence, and that the object of my visit was not so much to obtain any new light for my own satisfaction as for others; believing that, if I could see a *spirit* face so clearly as to be willing to affirm to its identify, it might be the means of causing some others to break away from the trammels of early education and habit, and investigate the subject for themselves. I was therefore careful to say nothing to compromise my object; and, further than the bestowal of a few words of encouragement and sympathy upon the *medium,* I said nothing, until several days after my arrival at Moravia, in connection with the foregoing *spirit* communications.

"On the last day, the 28th, the manifestations were somewhat better, both in the dark and light circles, than they had been, as was said, for some weeks. Several hands and arms were plainly exhibited, both outside and immediately within the cabinet, some of which were acknowledged as my wife's and daughters'. What purported to be my own mother, showed herself so that I could clearly see her plain Quaker bonnet, with cap beneath, but not her face distinctly enough to recognize it. Others present – whose eyesight was stronger than mine – described the features, however, as very much resembling hers. She also spoke audibly for a minute or two, very sensibly and characteristically, but not in her natural voice, but like one speaking through a trumpet – which might have been the case, as her face was not visible whilst speaking. Although I felt no doubt of her identify, and so expressed myself, she seemed disappointed that I could not see her more plainly, and made repeated efforts to bring her face further forward into the light. *(I regretted that I had not brought an opera-glass with me, which might have assisted my vision.)*

"On the forenoon of the next day, the 29th, my mother showed herself again, in the bonnet and cap, but I was still unable to distinguish her features so as to recognize them, although I had no doubt, as before, of her identity.

"At the next *séance* it was clearly the face of my dear sister Emily, every lineament of which was shown with the utmost and unmistakable distinctness. When young, she fell against the stove and cut quite a gash in her cheek *(and always carried the scar)*; the scar was now shown as plain as in the earth-life. I asked several questions, and in every instance got perfectly satisfactory and truthful answers, either by the nod of her head, or by the motion of the hands that were shown through the aperture in the partition. In spite of my best effort to control my emotions, tears of joy and gratitude flowed, as I knew it was a reality. I felt as though heaven was very near earth. If all could see their friends as distinctly as I saw my sister, there would be no doubt of immortality.

"Audible voices were frequently heard during the *séances.* Arms and hands were shown plainly, distinctly, two exhibiting arms above the elbow. Four hands were shown at one time. I have given a truthful statement of a portion of the wonders shown to myself and ten others. I presume the others present saw as plainly as I did.

"Besides showing her face in the light, my mother came several times in the dark *circles,* and manifested her presence by patting my head or hand with hers, or by speaking sometimes at considerable length in an audible, though not her natural earth-voice. At one time, she seemed to stand close by in front of where I was sitting and, with a mother's affectionate partiality, said, in a distinct whisper, "Thomas, my son, I am with you in all your good works." It would take too much space to describe even a tenth of the manifestations I witnessed at the score and more *seances* I attended at Moravia; I will therefore just refer to a few of the incidents that occurred, and hasten to conclude with the narrative of some that more particularly related to my own *spirit* family.

"One of the most active and efficient controlling *spirits* of both the dark and light circle at Moravia, is an Indian squaw called <u>Honto</u>. She frequently spoke very sensibly, though characteristically, of her Indian origin. On one occasion, while delivering quite a lengthy discourse in clear and forcible language, she took pride in exhibiting a beautiful scarlet blanket that was richly trimmed and ornamented with beads more brilliant than glass or even diamonds.

"Some of the *spirits* who spoke had passed from earth under the belief that there was no future state of existence, while others were imbued with the theological idea of a fiery hell. All such gratefully acknowledged their former error, and joined with others in hearing testimony to the fact, substantially, that no mere form of worship or belief can help to prepare any human being for a happy entrance into the *spirit*-world; and that the status mortals attain to on passing to the higher life is in conformity with the freedom and expansion of their minds – the good works they have done from unselfish motives, and the degrees of charity, sympathy and love they have manifested and exercised in their intercourse with their fellow-creatures on earth.

"On inspecting the cabinet at Moravia, I saw, at the first glance, that the aperture would not admit of such a manifestation as this; but the circumstance did not disconcert me in the least, having learned through experience that the *spirits* of mortals are – except in degree – no more infallible or omniscient in one sphere of existence than in another.

"The hands and arms that were shown at the aperture, unlike the faces, were always plain and distinct. On an occasion early after my arrival, wherein several hands of different sizes were passed by in the inside of the cabinet, one of them held a flower which I thought I recognized; but, to be sure, I asked a lady who sat beside me what it was. She promptly replied, "a lily." I than asked if the hand holding it was meant for me; and it was shown again in a token of assent. During my stay, this manifestation was repeated several times; and I have no doubt that the hand with the lily in it was, as it purported to be, my daughter Anna's, and one or more of the smaller hands her sister

Mary's. My wife also threw her arms full length, with hand clasped, out of the aperture on several occasions, always in a nightdress, which I suppose was meant to represent that she wore, in her last sickness. The sleeves were uniformly buttoned close to the hand; and I am sure the the exhibition could not have been more natural – including the folds and drapery of the garment – had she made a like manifestation before her departure from earth-life.

"From the first, I had been careful, for obvious reasons, not to mention my wife's or daughter's name. At a *séance* where there was an attempted demonstration at the aperture, so feeble that I could neither see nor hear distinctly anything that transpired. I was rather startled upon hearing a lady who had but recently arrived, observe, "She says 'Fanny Hagard'!" On asking the lady to repeat the name, she did the first, and said the last sounded something like "Hagard." On another occasion, a small star, enveloped in a mist-like halo, passed slowly upward from the bottom of the aperture, and disappeared at the top. This was twice repeated; and, upon my asking that it might show itself again if it was meant to represent my wife, it did so instantly, and remained stationary for a short time before its final disappearance. This was a beautiful manifestation, of which none present could know the full significance but myself. For the last fifteen years, my wife has been accustomed to draw a star, through some automatic and writing *mediums* I sat with, to announce her presence. It appears to be the name she is called by in *spirit*-life. Often, too, when I sit with trance or clairvoyant *mediums,* they will say, "Your star is here."

"Finally, my wife's repeated arduous but unavailing efforts became oppressive to me, and I told her repeatedly – sometimes directly, as she attempted to show herself, and at other times through *Rosa* or the controlling *spirit* of the *medium* present – that I was fully satisfied of her presence, and hoped she would not distress herself further on my account.

"Hitherto I had only attended the regular *seances,* the conditions of which were constantly being changed by the daily introduction of new and not always perfectly harmonious visitors. I had come to the conclusion that my staying longer could be of no avail, and proposed leaving Moravia.

"After she came out of trance, Mary Andrews described a lady *(answering to my wife)* who she said was writing something for me against a projection in the wall of the room, very near where I sat. On my asking her to tell me what the purport was, she read it off as follows: "Thomas, stay two days longer, and I think I can show myself to you." I asked her to intimate to my wife that I would cheerfully comply with her request, which she did.

"On the next day, after the two usual *seances* were closed, Mrs. Keeler, Mrs. Gibbs, Mr. Hoyt and myself held our private *séance.* The light was no sooner extinguished, than we perceived a marked and favorable change in the manifestations. The little stars that were wont to appear in the preliminary dark circle at most of the *seances,* were much brighter and more numerous than usual, and played about us with uncommon vivacity. *(Mr. Keeler subsequently told me that he had seen such little stars gradually expand and assume the appearance of human faces.)* The accompanying *spirit*-voices were also remarkably strong and distinct. We were assured by a guardian *spirit* of the *medium,* that, if a harmonious company, such as the one then present, could be convened for a few consecutive days, the manifestations would become far more powerful and vivid than any we had witnessed.

"My own mother came, and, as usual, identified herself to my satisfaction, in both the dark and light *circles.* My wife, also, exhibited her arms, full length, clothed in their usual drapery, but in a more desponding attitude than heretofore, they being bent and thrown upward, with the pale, attenuated hands tightly clasped, as if in earnest supplication or prayer. I thought I discerned the meaning she intended to convey, and what little renewed hopes I had entertained of her being able to show her features to me distinctly, almost entirely faded from the my mind. Several delicately formed hands, of different sizes, that looked as plain and real as if in earth-life, were passed by the aperture, just within the cabinet, one of them holding the customary lily. On this occasion, its petals exactly resembled those of the water-lily, and were of the most glistening white. These were for a considerable time turned in a full-blown point of view directly toward us, but with some of the petals so arranged as to hide the axial or seed bud. It looked so real and tangible that it seemed as if I might reach forth my hand and grasp it.

(As far as my own experience enabled me to determine, the spirit-hands at Moravia have none of the cold and velvet-like feeling usual in such phenomena, but were so natural that their touch could not be distinguished from the hands of persons in earth-life.)

"This was the last day of the two, on one of which my wife had notified me she hoped to be able to show her face to me.

"Both the morning and afternoon public circles on that day, though unusually large, were quite good. Several faces were shown very distinctly, and other manifestations occurred highly interesting.

After "Home, Sweet Home" had been twice sung, I asked that "Oft in the Still Nigh" *(a favorite melody of my wife's when in earth-life)* might be sung. Several stanzas were sung by the ladies present, in which a sweet feminine spirit voice joined in, though I failed to recognize it as that of my wife.

Immediately I felt a gentle and distinct pressure on my forehead, but whether made by her fingers or lips, I could not determine."

(Although much has been left out in the telling ... as it relates to others in the 'circle' who saw their loved ones and heard them also, one such episode follows: "In the light circle that followed, Albert and Thomas, two sons of Mr. Benjamin Fish, showed their faces and talked with their father. They were fully recognized. Albert, in referring to the doubts he had of a future state of existence when in earth-life, said, "We still live!" Mr. Fish's deceased wife came and showed herself as she looked in early womanhood. It was asked if she meant to show her features as they appear in spirit-life. To this she nodded assent, and disappeared, but immediately returned, looking as when passed from earth at the age of seventy.)

"Although I was conscious that my wife, aided by her *spirit*-friends, was exerting herself to the utmost to perfect the necessary conditions to show herself plainly to me, I had but little hope she would succeed, when suddenly, toward the last of the *séance,* I saw a face gradually developing or approaching the aperture, that I soon unmistakably recognized as hers. She seemed highly gratified at the recognition, and so expressed herself, looking as natural as in earth-life. I said, "It is enough; Fanny, I want no more; I am now fully satisfied!" Upon this, she thrust her face partly out of the aperture, and said, in a clear, loud whisper, "We have tried hard, Thomas, to make myself plain to you, and I thank God that we have succeeded!" My wife was within six feet of where I sat, and I saw her lips move as distinctly and naturally whilst she was speaking as I ever saw them in earth-life. Overcome with joyful emotion, I said, "Kiss me, darling!" whereupon her hand was twice raised to her lips as she threw me two kisses.

"Besides this, my wife has, on some occasions, shown herself very distinctly to me whilst in sleep, but always in a shadowy form, something analogous to the photograph. Again: For a year or more before my daughter Anna passed away, her mother repeatedly assured both her and myself that she would show herself to her before she passed from earth-life. This occurred, with wonderful distinctness, some few days before Anna died. I was present at the time. My daughter was lying on a lounge, and suffering intensely from spasmodic pain that periodically assailed her. I held one of her hands in mind, and her little brother and one or more of her sisters stood near by. Suddenly her countenance changed. The pain had entirely left her; and, with a radiant face, she looked beyond the side of the sofa, and said, "Why, Pa! There is mother! There is Aunt Gertrude, too!" She described them as standing in a beautiful forest, amidst flowers and shrubbery that hid their persons below the waist. I put several questions to my wife, which she answered satisfactorily by signs. The vision was perfectly enchanting to my sick daughter, who had no fear of death after wards, but looked cheerfully forward to it as a welcome messenger to waft her to her *spirit*-home and the others mentioned, was shadowy!

"Then it was, indeed, that I could comprehend the full significance of the tender emotions I had so often witnessed at Moravia, on the meeting of the living with loved friends that were dead, but "alive again"; and as my heart swelled with inexpressible gratitude toward the great, loving Parent of humanity, my tongue involuntarily exclaimed, "Surely, if there is a heaven on earth, it is here!

"Before this crowning proof, my spiritual experiences had banished all doubts from my mind as regards a future state of existence; but now, even belief that had passed into knowledge was doubly confirmed: the keystone was placed in the arch, from whence I know it never will or can be wrenched away. I had, at last, obtained all I sought for. I had looked upon the resurrected spirit-face of a loved one, the identity of whose features I am not only willing to affirm to, under the pains and penalties of perjury, before any assemblage of mortals or tribunal on earth, but, if need be, swear to it, on peril of my salvation, before the assembled hosts of heaven and judgment-seat of God."

ABOUT THE AUTHOR – Thomas R. Hazard

According to Sir Arthur Conan Doyle, "Thomas R. Hazard evidently knew the importance of ensuring the right conditions and the right type of sitters for any kind of investigation. He understood the importance of the attendance of any person or persons whose presence he deemed might conflict with the harmony and good order of the spirit circles."

If you do a search on Hazard's name, you will find the above quote on their http site: www.spiritualist.tv/spiritualism/history/vol1chapter14.html. You will also find the entire text of Sir Arthur Conan Doyle's book: *"The History of Spiritualism – Volume I"* on that same website!

EARLY LIFE

Hazard was born on January 3, 1797 in the village of South Kingstown, Rhode Island, the second-eldest son of textile industrialist Rowland Hazard and fifth-great-grandson of Thomas Hazard. At twelve, Thomas enrolled in the Friends' School at West Town, Pennsylvania but left to assist in the operation of the family's wool carding manufactures at Peace Dale. After a gift of two ewes sparked his interest in agriculture and livestock, Hazard acquired the nickname "Shepherd Tom."

In 1838 he married Frances Minturn, daughter of New York merchant Jonas Minturn. The couple had five children.

SOCIAL REFORM

In 1844, Hazard became one of the original twenty-three incorporators of the Rhode Island Hospital for the Insane, later Butler Hospital. The facility was the first of its kind in the state; responsibility for the care of destitute and mentally handicapped citizens at the time fell largely upon local governments.

Owing to his extensive record as an outspoken champion of the rights of the "insane poor," Hazard was appointed by the state to conduct a survey of Rhode Island's poor houses and insane asylums. *The Report on the Poor and Insane in Rhode Island: Made to the General Assembly at its January Session, 1851* provided a detailed census of *"insane paupers"* at thirty-three local facilities. The abuse of disabled Rhode Islanders in rural localities exposed in the report helped abolish state policies which treated mental illness as a crime.

Hazard was also a committed anti-slavery activist and published dozens of tracts in support of the <u>American Colonization Society</u> and the <u>Republic of Liberia</u>. From 1840 to 1841 he served as a Vice President of the ACS. Other causes for which he labored included the abolition of the death penalty in Rhode Island and public education.

SPIRITUALISM

Following the death of his wife in 1854, Hazard became interested in *spiritual communication* and began visiting *mediums* in Providence and Boston.

After two of his daughters died of tuberculosis and a third drowned herself in a river on the family's property, he dedicated himself exclusively to the defense of *mediumship*. His works on Spiritualism include:

- *Eleven Days at Moravia* (1873)

- *Blasphemy: Who Are the Blasphemers? The "Orthodox" Christians, or "Spiritualists"?* (1872)

- *Modern Spiritualism Scientifically Explained* (1875)

Hazard's Other Works   (1870-1880)

Hazard authored books of local folklore: *Recollections of Olden Times*; *Rowland Robinson of Narragansett and His Unfortunate Daughter*; *Genealogies of the Robinson, Hazard and Sweet Families of Rhode Island* ; *The Johnnycake Papers of "Shepherd Tom"*; and *Together with Reminiscences of Narragansett Schools of Former Days*. The latter became the subject of controversy when Dr. Leroy Vaughn used the work as evidence of Thomas Jefferson's African Heritage. The *Thomas Jefferson Foundation* has since dismissed these claims.

"VOICES FROM THE GRAVE"

A Chicago Times news reporter – Mr. Perry – came to
Moravia in 1874 with the intent of "exposing the *medium,
Mary Andrews*" but after the first "two unsatisfactory
seances," he witnessed three that convinced him of her
credibility. What follows are the three articles of what he
witnessed.

*(It was from the text of what he witnessed at the three
seances that the author wrote the play, "Circles" which was
performed in 2002, on March 29th and 30th at the Sylvan
Masonic Lodge #41, Moravia, New York. The play was
directed by Bourke Kennedy, the co-founder of the Auburn
Player's Community Theater Inc.)*

CASCADE, Cayuga Co., New York, Nov. 18, 1874. I saw a
queer advertisement the other day in The Religion-
Philosophical Journal. Said advertisement was to the
effect that John and Mary Andrews would be happy to see
their friends and patrons at the Cascade house, on the
short of Owasco lake; offering, as inducement to visitors,
good air, good boating, good fishing, and good news from
the spirit world! Can you imagine a more enticing
blending of the carnal and the spiritual? I couldn't and so
I am here to try my luck in the lake though I don't expect
to catch much; my fishing ground shall be the "vastly
deep, and I'll angle for angles!"

Cascade is a station on the Southern Central Railroad, just
at the head of Owasco lake, thirteen miles south of
Auburn. The number of houses in the place is one – at
once depot, hotel, post office, telegraph office, and
temple of Epiphenomena (Robert Dale Owen will tell you
what the last word means: I believe he is the patentee).
This eclectic establishment is a three story wooden
structure, painted white, and built in the usual summer

resort style. It stands near the margin of the lake. Back of it, just across the railroad track, rises a steep hill, down the rocky face of which tumbles the little waterfall which gives rise to the name of the place.

The Spiritualistic manifestations which I came to investigate, as a representative of The Times, are simply a continuation of those which for several years took place at Moravia. (The last named place is four miles further south, on the Southern Central Railroad and is a pleasant town of 2,000 people.)

The character of the phenomena, as begun at Moravia and continued at Cascade, has been exceedingly various, but the most remarkable manifestations that have taken place have been of the same class as those at the house of the Eddys, in Vermont; that is, purported materialization of spirit forms and faces. About three years ago, the excitement here was at its height. The New York Sun sent a correspondent here, and published several articles on the subject, and Mr. Hazard of Boston, wrote a pamphlet entitled, "Eleven Days at Moravia" – the nearest approach to full account that I have met with. But there is material for volumes, rather than letters and pamphlets. It is much to be regretted that some of our scientific investigators have not had time to examine the matter and keep a record of these startling phenomena. They certainly would have got facts enough to keep them classifying the rest of their lives. The recent Eddy and "Katie King" seances have perhaps distanced the Moravia circles in some respects; but, taking into consideration the circumstances under which the latter originated, and their long continuance without the discovery of the slightest trickery, they are certainly worthy of thorough investigation. That such investigation should be made

without bias is self-evident, I mean to argue neither for
nor again the spiritual hypothesis. But I want to say a
word to the critical reader, at the outset. When I speak of
an apparition, I may omit to call it a "so-called spirit", or a
"pretended spirit" and simply say "spirit". We will put it
on the simple ground that it is a saving of words to leave
out the terms with which our over curious skepticism is
apt to qualify the nomenclature of the faithful. If we
consider that nobody is committed by the avoidance of
these circumlocutory forms of expression, why then it
can't do any harm, you know.

The first two circles after my arrival were unsatisfactory.
Remembering my experiences of two years ago, I almost
began to fear that I should not find anything worth
reporting. Meanwhile I became perfectly familiar with
the circle room, and am prepared to describe it in detail.
You must know, then, that it is a room about eighteen feet
square, and ten feet high, in the third story, and looks very
much like any other room of the same size in a country
hotel. The floor is covered with matting, and the walls
with cheap paper. I tried hard to find a trap door or a
false face, for I knew that either would be sure to make
me my fortune as an exposer of Spiritualism; but none
existed, so far. Two of the walls of the room are next to
out of doors, and each has a window both of which
windows are covered to exclude the light by thin boards
and black oil cloth. I satisfied myself that no confederate
could get in through said windows by any possibility. The
other two walls are next to sleeping rooms, which I
entered, finding them to be supplied with the quota of
chamber furniture, and nothing more. I found that these
inner partitions were of the same thickness as ordinary
partitions, and discovered no sliding panels or secret
closets worth speaking of. Over the room is the

garret, and every one can witness the emptiness of it by climbing up the step ladder in the hall.

The furniture of the room consists of a dozen or twenty rush bottomed chairs, a wood stove, a small stand with a lamp on it, and a rough paper screen about two feet square and the cabinet. The latter is simply a box (lacking only the bottom), about nine feet in length by seven in height, and three in depth. It is made of chestnut and the sides vary in thickness (being paneled) from half an inch to an inch. The furniture of the cabinet is one small chair. You go within, and the most rigid scrutiny fails to disclose anything but the smooth sides of the chestnut box, the matted floor and the chair. The cabinet stands against he wall, but I got behind it far enough to see that there were no hidden means of communication with the next room. The front of the cabinet has a door with an opening in the upper part, about one and a half by two feet, which opening is covered on the inside by a black velveteen curtain. And now I believe I have told you all that is necessary.

I ought perhaps, before leaving the subject of the cabinet, to say that the circle room and cabinet are always open for inspection.

As I have already said, the first results of my present visit were decidedly discouraging. In the third séance, however, the shining shore began to brighten up a little, and although the séance was not specially remarkable in itself, I will give you my notes of it, on account of its close connection with the one immediately following. We will call it ....

S E A N C E   N O. 1

We entered the circle room at 10 o'clock yesterday
forenoon. We found the requisite number of chairs for the
party arranged in front of the aperture of the cabinet,
about six feet back, in precisely the way they fix them for
the first part of a minstrel performance. I took the place
usually assigned to the Bones. The corresponding
position at the other end of the line was ably filled by
Judge E. Between were two ladies of the judge's family,
and two other ladies. The medium came in, fastened the
door, pinned her shawl over the crack to exclude every
ray of light, put out the light of the lamp on the stand,
directed us to join hands, and sat down in a chair by the
side of the cabinet door, directly facing us. Thus began
the "dark circle", as they call it. You know they always
have to sing to bring the bright angels from the heavenly
shores. The judge suggested that we should open with a
song. He lit on the grand old air from the "Bohemian Girl"
– the long metre Coxology! As soon as he had reached
"Father, Son and Holy Ghost", he hastened to say, "Now I
don't consider that orthodox at all; I apply it to
Spiritualism and ration good sense." "Everyone seems to
like that tune," said one of the ladies. "Oh, yes,"
responded the judge, "there's such a beautiful sentiment
in it you know." Then they sang the "Sweet Bye and Bye".
During the performance of this piece, I felt the patting of
invisible fingers on my knee and head very distinctly. I
ought to mention there that Mrs. Andrews always joins
lustily in the singing, so as to show that she does not do
the patting. Others said they were touched at the same
time I was. The next place on the bill was "Why Does The
White Man Follow My Path?" a solo by Mrs. Andrews,
chorus by the entire company. After which the judge
suggested "John Brown's Body". The hint was not
complied with, much to my regret. I had heard so much

about that tune that I had a curiosity to hear it. "When I
Can Read My Title Clear" was substituted, during which
there was some sharp tappings on the lamp chimney. The
judge asked if it was his son who rapped, and three raps
responded ... yes. He seemed to be satisfied with the
identity, and asked several questions, which were replied
to by raps. Then "Come To Jesus" was suggested. The
company accordingly came. Then followed a tedious
amount of singing of the same general character as the
foregoing, during which nothing happened of any note.
Finally we heard a voice, apparently coming from mid-air,
several feet above the tops of our heads. Someone said,
"Why that's Dr. Baker", and the voice by the name of Dr.
Baker proceeded to inform us in husky but clearly
audible accents that there was not sufficient "life and
animation" in the circle for the spirits to work on. "But,"
says he "bring all these 'ere people up here tonight, and
we'll have a good circle." And we broke up on the
strength of the doctor's promise.

I cannot conveniently carry along the thread of my true
story any further, without introducing you to Dr. Baker. I
shall have to tax your credulity a little, I fear, but I have
taken pains to authenticate the story, and I am satisfied of
its genuineness. Perhaps the logical way to begin the
narrative would be to say that once upon a time a face
appeared at the aperture of Mrs. Andrews' cabinet,
purporting to be a materialization of the disembodied
spirit of Dr. Baker, but that would consume too much
valuable time; so (bearing in mind what I have said about
not committing anybody by these unqualified
expressions) we will just say that Dr. Baker, of
Kelloggsville, N.Y., in the vicinity of Moravia, has
appeared scores of times at Mrs. Andrews' circles, looking
so much like he did when on earth that all his old

acquaintances in the neighborhood had no difficulty in recognizing him. He was a man of marked individuality. He was a lover of horses, a fast driver, a man of remarkable energy and pluck in every department of life. His old partner in the medical profession was not only skeptical, but really abusive on the subject of Spiritualism. But he came to the circle one day and went home a firm believer; for Dr. Baker showed his face and talked to him for a long time. He descended so far from his heavenly altitude as to reproach his old associate with selling a favorite horse that he had let him have – "Old Gray" – the trade having been consummated that very morning. The doctor (this is the angel doctor) is still a constant visitor at Mrs. Andrew's circles, and, it is reported that he has managed to make his positive character as strongly felt as when he was on this side of Jordan. He has a good deal of say about the management of the circles, and often comes in sharp conflict with George Jackson, who claims to be the real master of ceremonies, but rules with a milder sway than the doctor. I have no authentic information that Jackson has ever been identified, but he claims that he lived while on our plant at Flint, Michigan, and followed some minor occupation in life.

SEANCE NO. 2

It began at 8 o'clock last evening. Our number was augmented to the extent of two ladies and two gentlemen, constituting us a circle of ten. The method of procedure was precisely the same as it was in the morning, but the results were much more satisfactory. In fact, if the judge had not sprung that irrepressible doxology on us two or three times – I swear to two – I should be prepared to say that we had an exceedingly lively time. In the whole, the music was very good, for one of the new ladies played a guitar for us, and sang two or three solos in fine style. An invisible hand swept the strings of the guitar with tremendous force several times while she was playing. It was very distinct to my perception, for I sat next to the lady.

The judge was one of the end men, as before. Next to him sat two young ladies. We were singing the third time, I believe, when lady number one burst out with a yell like a wild cat. "Go away from me you big Injun!" she pleaded in tones of unfeigned terror. And she laughed and then screeched in regular alternation. "Why he's taking my hair down!" says she; "he's taking my earrings out" and we hear them drop on the floor. Pretty soon lady number two began to complain in a hysteric way that her own back hair was being mussed by some invisible being from the realms above (anyhow that's a fair abstract of what she said). And when at last the invisible voice cried, "Strike a light!" … the request was complied with and the ladies aforesaid were discovered with disheveled tresses, and blushing, giggling faces, their hands locked fast with those of their neighbors, who declared they had not released them for an instant. If Mrs. Andrews did it, she must have done it with a pole, for she was at least eight feet from these ladies, and we could tell that her position was unchanged, by the sound of her voice; for she was singing like a Boston jubilee every blessed minute. That a lady would do such a thing herself as to remove her switches and other personal adornments in a miscellaneous company is a hypothesis that is too slanderous to be worthy of notice.

The light was struck, as I before observed, it being turned up to about the usual height, and so placed behind the screen that the circle was left comparatively dark, the light falling on the black velvet curtain covering the aperture. Immediately after the lighting of the lamp, Mrs. Andrew went and sat down in her chair inside of the cabinet. And thus began our first light circle. And just at this point in my statement I observe an excellent opportunity to edge in a little sentiment.

You all know the intense interest and breathless expectation that await the rising of the curtain and the beginning of the first act. But suppose that instead of awaiting the appearance of your favorite Southern or Jefferson, as Dundeary or Rip, you were anticipating the debut of a being from another world, clothed in the habiliments of his whilom mortality, how do you think you'd feel? Wouldn't a gentle feeling of solemnity steal over your awe stricken spirit? Your expectancy might be strongly mingled with doubt and distrust, but I am very sure that the bare possibility of talking face to face with a disembodied spirit, specially reincarnated for the occasion would shorten your breath and arouse every faculty of your mind into intense activity. At any rate, that's about the way it was with our little company last night. Every eye was turned with keenest scrutiny toward the little black velvet curtain. We saw it move as if a breath of air was lifted far enough to leave a triangular opening of ten or twelve inches in height. The sharpest eyed of the circle exclaimed, "There's a face!" Gradually the outlines became distinguishable to all, the face approached nearer to the opening of the cabinet, and "George Jackson" was the almost universal exclamation. The face appeared to be that of a man of middle age, with regular features and a stout full beard sprinkled with gray.

Before going further, I shall have to go back and pick up a

thread or two. The lady who played the guitar had near
the close of the dark circle, played and sung a comic
medley at the request of a gentleman present who had
heard it before. When the face that purported to be the
materialization of a portion of the deceased Jackson had
advanced to the opening, as I have narrated, it turned
itself half round, being at the time partly projected
out of the aperture, and looked the lady alluded to full in
the face. The lips moved, and the presence said: "Don't
sing such songs as that last one you sang; not that there is
any harm in them, but they leave a feeling of levity that is
unfavorable." The voice was husky and tremulous, but
distinctly audible to all. The lady begged pardon and
said she would not offend again. The voice continued:
"Friends you are very patient. It has been very hard for
us to materialize for the past few days. The cabinet is new
(it had been in use only two weeks), the room has been
used for other purposes of late and the magnetic
conditions have been such that we have met with extreme
difficulty in our efforts. Be patient; the time is but short
when we shall be able to produce better manifestations
than we have ever given you." He then answered some
inquiries from members of the circle, and concluded by
assuring us of the reality of the life beyond the grave, and
the near approach of its indisputable demonstration. He
emphasized his remarks by peculiar motions of the head,
and at such times would frequently thrust his face almost
entirely out of the aperture into the full blaze of the light
which fell upon it from behind the screen; and, to be
candid, I must confess that to me, at a distance of
probably six feet, it looked astonishingly like the real
flash and blood.

After "Jackson" retired,the curtain raised again, and "How
do you do, Dr. Baker?" was the simultaneous inquiry of

several voices. The face that called forth with a burst of recognition, edged itself in sidewise in front of the curtain and was accompanied by an uplifted hand of a very peculiar appearance. From where I sat I could not see the face as soon as most of the others, but I saw the hand distinctly. I said to myself, "You're sold now, anyway" for the hand was as small as a child's, and apparently deformed at that. I learned afterward that it was a facsimile of the hand of the mortal Dr. Baker, and that its peculiar appearance was the effect of an injury received by being thrown from a buggy, I believe. In an instant after the appearance of the hand, the face came out with startling clearness, and was distinctly seen by all. He responded to our salutations in a rough, husky voice, the articulation being not quite so distinct as Jackson's, but some how louder. To give every word that he uttered would take at least a solid half column of The Times. He remained at least, a full half hour. The face was rounder than that of the previous apparition; the head was covered with a mass of white hair, combed so straight across the forehead than at first I thought it was a handkerchief bound round his temples. The chin bristled with a heavy beard of snowy whiteness. As he projected his face from time to time through the aperture, the light fell full upon the beard, and you could see the struggling hairs standing out in every direction with the utmost distinctness. But the doctor's talk was the most remarkable event of the evening. He first turned to the lady vocalist and brought up the comic song question again. Said he, "I like that song, and I'm glad you sung it. Jackson is always showing himself in where he's not wanted."

By this time our solemn feelings had substantially subsided, and we smiled so that you could hear it. The doctor went on; "We all gave have our different dispositions and likes and dislikes when we are on earth and when we go to the other side, we're all the same. Some like one thing and some like another."

"You think you have better taste than your friend Jackson in the music line?" I ventured to ask. "Certainly," was the reply; "I don't like those old Methodist tunes; I want something lively and cheerful. That's the way to look at it – the cheerful way. When the clouds look black, don't look at 'em; look right on beyond, where it's all bright, and move right on."

I requested the privilege of asking a question of the doctor. He said I might ask two if I wanted. I had in mind at the time a rumor that had recently come to me, that of the controlling spirits, while the manifestations were at Moravia, declared that a single spirit had power to take on various temporary bodies, and admitted that some of these phenomena had been produced in that deceptive way, seeming to present a variety of personalities, when in reality it was only a single spiritual juggler who produced them all. So I asked if any of the diakka class of spirits had power to materialize any other forms than their own? He promptly answered by propounding the conundrum: "Could anybody get a picture of you but yourself?" When further questions on the same general subject, he said he did not see how any spirit could show Dr. Baker's face but himself; he had never seen such a thing done, and didn't believe it could be otherwise.

In answer to questions in regard to the power of spirits to assume these temporary bodies for purposes of identification, he said that it was easier for them to show themselves as they were at just the time when they left their earthly bodies; but they sometimes had the power to go back farther. In regard to the composition of the face shown at the cabinet window, he said: "We get these elements from you who sit in the circle, you know. There's a big man over there we can draw a great deal from."

"Where do the faces go to when they disappear?" said one. "When you look in the mirror and see your picture, where does that go when you go away?" was the conundrumistic rejoinder. He said we must sit up straight and keep our feet flat on the floor, and keep perfectly still while we were in the circle. "You wouldn't get a very good picture of yourself at a gallery if you should shuffle around while the artist was trying to take you."

At one point in the conference meeting the ladies besought the doctor in a perfect chorus to give them "tests".

He said he couldn't come there and fool away his time with such nonsense, but he answered some of the most urgent inquiries of the truth seekers who were anxious to know if their grandmothers and grandfathers were present, and finally wound up with the pertinent inquiry if there were not some others who wanted to know if there was an old man or an old woman by the side of them? Several times he said, "Well, I guess I'll have to drive one, but some new question would be broached, and he would answer it. He gave one of the girls of the house who was present a severe scolding for an impatient remark she had made during the day. "Did you hear that?" said she. "Why certainly; didn't you hear that old pan rattle?" "Yes," was the answer. "Well, that was me," said he; "and I shall come every time you don't behave yourself. You must always count to four before you speak." (To make

the connection complete, I ought to state that the raps on
the tin pan in the kitchen were heard by several others,
and it was matter of common remark in the house long
before the circle began. I had heard of it several hours
before.) Then the old fellow turned around to the
medium in the corner of the cabinet, and gave her
particular fits for some impropriety of conduct in regard
to her children. And then he scolded people in general
for their luxurious habits, anathematized stoves, and
cracked up fire-places; urged the importance of keeping
the feet warm and the head cool, gave a lady a
prescription for catarrh, and acted – in a word –
exceedingly like a rough, common sense old physician of
the last generation.

So you have had enough of Dr. Baker, I recon. If he was
only Mary Andrews, with a white wig and beard on, then
all I have to say is that she has a talent for histrionic art
that would enable her, with very slight culture, to wear
with perfect propriety the crown that the great Cushman
has so recently and frequently abdicated, for, although I
have seen manifestations of this class where there was
even less opportunity for trickery than there is in Mrs.
Andrews' cabinet, yet I must confess that I never
encountered a purported spirit of such a vigorous
personality, and the psychological effect of which it is so
difficult for my obstinate professional skepticism to
overcome.

S E A N C E NO. 3

In my recent letter on the subject of the physical
manifestations taking place at Cascade, New York, I gave
some account of the history of the phenomena, together
with a synopsis of two seances which I attended during

my last visit.

I was present at several others afterward, but I will give you a report of only one of them, which was perhaps the most remarkable dark circle during my stay.

The usual preliminaries were gone through with; the persons present (about eight in number) were seated in a semi-circular line, facing the cabinet, hands were joined, the door fastened, and shawl was pinned over it, the light was extinguished, and the inevitable doxology was truck up. Hardly had we got "Praise Him Above, Ye Heavenly Host" out of our mouths, when the inevitable powers responded to the exhortation by hurling a chair against the wall behind us with such force as to leave the prints of the chair legs in the plastered wall to the depth of half an inch (as we found by subsequent investigation) and startled the ladies of the party into outbursts of hysterical terror. The chair was one of a row (numbering perhaps a dozen) that sat against the wall in the back part of the room, about eight feet in the rear of the circle. Well, who did it? Certainly no one in the circle could have thrown the chair without being instantly detected. No one could have left the circle without releasing the hand of at least one other person; six of the eight could not have left their positions without letting go the hands of two persons. The character of the persons composing the circle was not by any means such as to create the presumption of a conspiracy for purposes of deception. Indeed, the party was so small that is hardly conceivable that such an instantaneous movement could have been made by any one without discovery. Of course, the persons sitting at either end of the line could have left their places with the least danger of detection. As to the one of these, a delicate lady, I can testify personally, for I sat next to her, knew that she did not leave her seat, and believed, from her conduct the the time, that her nervous excitement at the mysterious noise was not only unfeigned, but really serious. As to the party at the other end (say eight or ten feet from where I sat), he was the leader of our ex tempore choir, and his voice sounded out loud and clear above all the others. In fact, in a company so small as ours, and arranged in such a fashion, it was easy to determine very nearly the position of each person by the sound of his voice. The medium, bear in mind, was sitting in front of the circle, not more than six feet from any of us, on the opposite side of the room from the disturbance, at least twelve feet from where it occurred. She is a pretty strong woman, but I don't really see how she could sling a chair over our heads, and strike the wall with the force indicated by conclusion. Besides, there was no chair to throw in that part of the room. If she got in behind us, and picked up a chair, and banged it against he wall, she must be a powerful ventriloquist, as well as a clever trickster; for, as far as human sense of hearing could judge, Mary Andrews' strong, clear voice never ceased during the time in question (say sixty seconds) to accompany us, from her chair in front of the soul-moving harmonies of the long-meter doxology. Somebody probably came in from the door, you may suggest, and raised the rumpus. That may be; not knowing, I couldn't say; but if that was the way of it, all I have to say is that the door was re-fastened on the inside and the shawl pinned over the crack between the door and the casing with marvelous secrecy and dispatch. Under the circumstance, I was certainly unwarranted in charging any one with confederacy in the matter. I have said more about occurrence than its intrinsic significance justified, I am aware; but I have stated the case thus fully for the purpose of showing that in this entire investigation, I have directed

my attention to all the bearings of each particular
phenomena in order to discover every possible solution
consistent with the purely human origin of the
manifestations.

But to return to the circle. The next was a display of tiny
meteoric lights in the air, several feet above our heads.
They came and went and moved about very much like
large sized lightning bugs. I noticed similar appearances
at several previous seances. They are said to appear at
times in rings and other varieties of form. These celestial
fireworks, so to speak, have the appearance of
phosphorescent lights. (I have recently learned, however
that a party of professors at Cornell University once
tested these 'celestial fireworks' by impregnating the air
of the circle room with certain chemicals in the presence
of which phosphorescent lights cannot be produced; and
yet these mysterious lights continued to shine as
frequently and as brilliantly as ever!)

Other phenomena of the séance were, sensations of
strong electric currents experienced by several of the
party, including myself, waves of hot and cold air, and at
times a cool breeze (felt by all, and greeted with
simultaneous exclamations of surprise) blowing right in
our faces with sufficient strength to lift the hair from our
foreheads. All these manifestations, bear in mind, took
place while all present, including the medium, were
engaged in singing, voices were heard, apparently just in
front of us, and a little above our heads. One of these
voices utter a few words in German in a very distinct
manner, and simultaneously a lady and gentleman sitting
next to me on the right, told us that they felt the touch of
invisible hands. Not withstanding the distinctness of the
tone, we were unable to catch all the words, on account of

our ignorance of the language, but "lieben sie gott" was clearly audible. The lady just referred to asked if the words were spoken to her, and there was no response; but when the gentleman next to her asked if the spirit of so and so was present, his knee was patted with a pat that amount to a pound! Another voice gave to Judge E. the full name of a man who, before his death was a well known official of the State of Pennsylvania, and added, "Thank God, I can come to you."

Other voices were heard, and other pattings were experienced. Many of these demonstrations gave a good deal of apparent satisfaction to persons present, but, as they were of substantially the same character as those already report, I should be needlessly repetitious were I to go over them in detail. So I will close right here the record of my direct, personal investigation of these puzzling phenomena.

CONCLUSION: The focus of popular attention at Moravia and Cascade has been mainly the appearances of faces, hands, and other portions of the human figure at the aperture of Mrs. Andrew's cabinet – faces of all shapes and sizes and colors and varieties of expression. The most ready response to the theory that these faces are materialization of angelic countenances is that they are false faces; and it was rumored in Moravia at one time that Mrs. Andrews had been returning from the city with a basket full of artificial faces and arms and hands! I did not learn, however that any of them were ever found on her premises. The apparitions seen by myself certainly do not look like false faces. Sometimes they are shown so far back from the aperture that there is hardly light enough to see their outlines. – Under such circumstances, of course, a false face manufactured by mortal hands might easily pass for a true face constructed by the art of higher spheres. It is fair to say, however, that these faces are projected out into the light so far that every feature, and even the very wrinkles of the face and the straggling hairs of the beard are distinctly visible. And the strangest of all ... the faces talk! The lips are sometimes seen to move, like those of the dying, when no sound come from them, but usually the voice, if there is any attempt to speak at all, is strong and audible though not very clear; there is generally a peculiar huskiness about the voice (as I have before remarked), as if the throat were clogged up, and the appearance is that of a person speaking with great difficulty.

Right here a story I've heard so often, from such a variety of sources, that I will venture to give it to you, although it is not a part of my personal knowledge.

One day, one of the visitors chanced to remark in a skeptical tone that "those who boasted materialization were only using false faces" and it was the face that called itself 'George Jackson' that responded by – opening his mouth wide, and disclosed a complete set of teeth, to all appearances, and (while the company waited in breathless silence) brought the upper and lower jaws together several times so forcibly that the sound could be heard all over the room, and said – "Does this look like a false face?" The teeth looked like teeth, and sounded like teeth, when they struck each other and there being no wide-awake skeptic present to find out whether or not they were false teeth, the matter was dropped.

But, after all, the main question is: Are the faces recognized? Are they really the faces of departed friends? This is the point where the fight is most fiercely contested by the skeptics and the believers. The former say that many people are weak minded and credulous, and self-deluded so that they see their deceased grandfathers on the slightest provocation, and fancy that the illustrious dead are ever subject to their call. And there is a great deal of cause for such criticism.

THE THEORY OF MORRIS KEELER

I had some curiosity to get the theory of Morris Keller in reference to these demonstrations. You remember that it was in his house near Moravia, New York, that the manifestations began, while Mary Andrews was a girl living with the Keelers. I went over to Moravia to see the old gentleman. I found him in the barn. He took me into the house, and I had a very interesting talk with him and his wife. Mr. Keeler is a very rotund specimen of mankind. If his old fashioned swallow-tail coat was a little slicker and the hayseed was out of his hair, he would pass for an alderman, as well as he does now for a granger. His countenance is a perpetual twinkle of jollity. His talk is quaint and original. His wife is as much too small as he is too large. Both are silver-haired and must be nearing four-score. They told me (what I had learned from other sources) that these manifestations were the result of years of patient investigation, and were a slow development. First came raps and table-moving; then lights and voices; and last ... faces and forms. The spirits promised this grand climax years before the faces came, they said; they also foresaw that the medium would leave the house and the manifestations cease for a time; but the faithful old couple have the fullest belief that the spirits have pledged their word to honor to return again and give them the blessing of their presence in a way tenfold more glorious and satisfactory than ever.

And so they hold their daily circles the same as when they had a house full of visitors, and calmly wait for the millennium – the time when the spirits will be visible to all eyes in the brightest light of day, in as full form and power of action as they were on earth. They broach their marvelous faith, not with fantastical vehemence, but with the calm and smiling air of invincible confidence. The simple faith of these white-haired old people is very touching. They stand on the brink of the grave, and look forward longingly, not to the time when they shall spread their wings and mount to heaven, but to the happy day when the angelic hosts will reign on earth! Well, it's an old faith, and I am sure we'll hope that the good time will come at last.

+ + + + + + + + + +

THE PLAY 'CIRCLES' WAS PERFORMED IN THE SYLVAN MASONIC LODGE IN MORAVIA ON FRIDAY AND SATURDAY, MARCH 29 AND 30, 2002. THOSE WHO PERFORMED IN THE PLAY INCLUDED: ALAN CLUGSTON, SAM TAMBURO, CHERI FARNSWORTH, MARK VENDETTI, JOHN HAIGHT, JOEL WEIRICK, SUE STOYELL, NANCY WEAVER AND COLLIN SULLIVAN. DURING THE INTERMISSION – SONGS OF THE ERA – WERE PERFORMED BY "THE MERRY MISCHIEF".

STAGE MANAGER: STEPHANIE BIELEJEC
TECHNICAL DIRECTOR: MARK BRUZEE
LIGHTS: WAYNE FULLER.

+ + + + + + + + + + + +
AMEN!

Made in the USA
San Bernardino, CA
10 August 2017